Acceptance

Acceptance

Passage into Hope

Miriam Pollard, OCSO

Michael Glazier
Wilmington, Delaware

About the Author

Sister Miriam Pollard is a member of the Cistercian Nuns of the Strict Observance, Mount Saint Mary's Abbey, Wrentham, Massachusetts 02903. Her other published works include *The Laughter of God.*

First published in 1987 by Michael Glazier, Inc., 1935 West Fourth Street, Wilmington, Delaware, 19805. ©1987 by Michael Glazier, Inc. All rights reserved. Library of Congress Catalog Card Number: 87-45004. International Standard Book Number: ACCEPTANCE: 0-89453-619-2, paper. Cover design by Ericka Hellwig. Printed in the United States of America.

*For Mother Angela
who lived, taught,
and rejoiced in hope.*

TABLE OF CONTENTS

Part Three: The Celebration of Limitation

Part Four: The How-To Section

Part Five: Ends and Beginnings

BEFORE THE BEGINNING

It's not much help to be told that God is the solution to your problems when he is one of them. He is, of course, a different problem to different people. Some do not—or do not want—to believe in God, and I am not here directly concerned with that trouble. But some believe and almost wish they couldn't, or at least that they could have another image of God in exchange for the one they're stuck with.

It's these I'm interested in; I'm going to presuppose belief in God and in the principle truths of faith, and talk about what happens to truth when it gets corroded by a set of emotional reactions which I think are common enough to mention. In fact, I suspect that a lot of the people who wouldn't want to try the temper of the spectre they address as God by bringing up the subject in conversation with him, have a number of the feelings I will be discussing.

The book is probably best thought of as a series of meditations set in more or less progressive order. It is not supposed to be raced through, and I have buried a few land mines here and there to blow off a foot if you try. Part One circles the difficulty, taking a look from different angles. The rest of the book is an effort to show that what looks like a spiritual mudslide can turn into a perfectly good road.

The book may be useful to people who have the problems, people who feel locked out of the hearts of friends who do, and even perhaps a few whose intellectual difficulties have emotional components. It may be reassuring as well to people whose belief is staggering for want of support from a consistent spiritual life. They may be encouraged to know how possible the spiritual life is even though it never seems to work right.

PART ONE
THE PROBLEM

BEGINNING

We come late.

Being born is not much of a beginning. Everything seems to have happened before we get there. The child in the womb is an articulation of something that began with the first flicker of material energy. By the time we begin our acquaintance with the world, history has happened, and the culture into which we are born has been established. Language is given us, shaper and restrictor of our thought.

Our brains and our bodies come with their particular set of characteristics. This temperament, this personality are given to me. I am not the sister or brother or the girl in school whose personality I would rather have than mine. (She is popular; she doesn't get into trouble.) The predispositions that will show through a lifetime of objective observations are asleep in us or walking around in the mental habits of other people. Our social setting and the psychological framework of those who will provide a first and formative interpretation of the world are already there ahead of us. So much is over before we get our chance. So much that is not ourselves determines how much of a chance we will get.

There is a reverently cheerful way to look at this, conclusions like those drawn by Donald Nicholl as he walked back through the years nature has turned to rock between the rim and the river of Grand Canyon:

> You start to reflect that the very eyes with which you are observing these wondrous evidences are themselves the result of millions of years of striving for light, ever since the first pin-hole eye appeared on those primitive marine creatures, the cephalopods. And you are the beneficiary of all that struggle for light, the heir to all that agony. And as you gaze at your hands or think of your ears or of your tongue, it takes your breath away to envisage the innumerable strivings that had to be attempted before you could see and touch and hear and taste and speak... You realize what an incredibly hard-won privilege it is simply to be a human being.[1]

The less cheerful outlook is the one you get after you've blown your chances for something you want, or stumbled and got hurt, or just read the evening paper—that stifling, enchained certainty that the world, and your self which is a thread in the fabric of the world, have been somehow robbed of the capacity to be what you would have them be.

It's not hard to realize that we are born into a narrow range of choice. The African baby riding its mother's back as she sows and weeds and hopes for rain may never get to choose at all. The rains may not come. The hot sky may write across another small life, "There was no time." The gap between what we want and what we can have may be large or small, depending on the day and the circumstance. The constriction into which our birth has dropped us and in which our life

---

[1]Donald Nicholl, *Holiness* (The Seabury Press, NY, 1981).

envelops us can be as entire as the pain from which Alan Paton's Stephen Kumalo cried,

> If I return to Indochene, do you know what I will preach there? That we are all lost here on this rock, that turns around the sun without meaning.[2]

or, as matter-of-fact as Emily Dickinson's

> Heaven is what I cannot reach!
> The apple on the tree
> Provided it so hopeless hang
> That heaven is to me.
>
> The color on the cruising cloud
> The interdicted ground
> Behind the hill, the house behind—
> There Paradise is found![3]

For Stephen, the possible horror of life had become more real than it does for most of us, and Emily's desires came back to her with clipped wings. She explored the limitations life imposed on her by imposing on herself the exterior limitations of space, and—in a woman's gesture of significance—of color. She chose to be the woman in white, whose feet for years passed back and forth on the same few hundred yards of earth. Even her use of language is famously compressed, a fierce celebration of the expansive power of brevity.

Paton's Stephen, as Paton's life, has found a loose board in the fence that enclosed him, and drawing us along, stumbles

[2]Alan Paton, *Cry the Beloved Country* (1948).

[3]Emily Dickinson, *Selected Poems and Letters of Emily Dickinson,* Ed. Robert N. Linscott (Doubleday Anchor, NY, 1959).

out onto a winding road. Emily meets us now at unexpected turns in our journey of the spirit. She knows, she has been there, she is the learner of seasons—seasons of nature and of the heart—the ponderer of impossible loves, the expression of what we almost do not know.

Resources are of many kinds. Sometimes the restrictions on our power of choice can be advantages. Life is often, after all, a matter of making the same few choices over and over again. When we weigh our capacities against our limitations at least two factors affect the balance. One is that if what we see around us is all there is, then the human situation is not encouraging. But if we believe there is more than we see, then what we believe has to make use of both resources and liabilities. That is part of the belief. It erases the necessity for full equipment. We're not so badly off; we have enough for the job.

The other consideration is a question: What then is the job? If our task is to change the world or even a particular portion of the world, nobody could call us stupid for getting discouraged. For all his rationality, talent, and goodness, what can Alan Paton do for South Africa? Emily Dickinson made her family's bread while her country fought the Civil War.

Yes, we do things. We help, we comfort, we heal and reshape and teach. We analyze, complain and criticize. But we do not feel very successful, at least if we're smart enough to spot the inadequacy of our solutions. And this is because successful reconstruction of the world or any part of it is not what we are born to, not what our resources and liabilities add up to. We are not asked for this, and not equipped for it. What we are asked for is to have a try at it, a good, consistent, unrelenting try. In Eliot's famous lines, "for us there is only the trying. The rest is not our business." [4]

But that is only part of the task. Or perhaps the trying is part of another task. When the world is so badly in need of fixing, and we ourselves are so badly in need of being lost in its healing, how shockingly selfish it can sound to say that our job is not fixing but searching, and the object of our search is ourselves. The task is me. My life is a journey in company with the invisible stranger who is myself; I must learn the mystery of who I am and be it.

This does not seem selfish to me—unoriginal, maybe, but not selfish—because the journey inward is at the same time the journey outward. And only by being what we really are can we wriggle out of the enchainment which we share with what we call the problem of the world. It is only in this search that we can serve, since otherwise we will be only one more chain around the world's neck, no matter how good our intentions. We will harness the objects of our compassion to our desire to be something we are not. Intentions are not enough. Indeed, they can be half the trouble.

But isn't there something wrong with having to spend a lifetime finding out what you need to know in order to begin? How can I be of use to the world if my usefulness depends on being something I don't yet know and won't sufficiently be until it's time to leave the world I want to help? "In my end is my beginning," but this is ridiculous. Is this what life is all

---

[4] T.S. Eliot, "Four Quartets," *Complete Poems and Plays* (Harcourt, Brace, Jovanovich, NY, 1963).

about? Hanging around until we can begin something just when it's time to leave?

Who am I? Can't I be told and start from there? The answer to that is yes and no. Yes, to some extent I can be told. There's a lot of information on the subject and a lot of ways by which we can absorb it. Some books concern themselves explicitly with the nature of human destiny—scriptural and liturgical texts, their commentaries, theology. Some books are, or may be, less explicit, they are heavy with implication— literature, poetry. But that is not all. We have music, dance, sculpture, architecture, painting. The natural world which tugs and presses at our senses is clamoring to tell us our name. Other people are dropping clues and drawing maps.

I can be told. I have been. So have you. We have been introduced to truth. And whenever we are tempted to despair of this learning process, we should take an hour from our activities and make our quiet way through some document in which we have been given access to the struggle, wisdom, and accomplishment of all the years we haven't had to live and without which we cannot make our own few years work out. The text could be sublime or simple, sacred or secular, words that draw us beyond our cramped environment or give us the comfort of another's understanding in face of a common hurt. From Plato to Shakespeare to *Charlotte's Web*, the Declaration of Independence or *Gift from the Sea* — we have only to put out a hand.

I think this is a good thing to do often, and although Scripture should be a daily companion, we could also use a painting, a photo, a videocassette of Nureyev and Fonteyn or Fred Astaire, a tree in the back yard or a letter from someone we love. It's only a matter of asking a few questions: What has this given me in knowledge and in the ability to live? What is it telling me now? Then we should rest in appreciative silence, present to this evidence that the world which was here before us is as much a source of beauty as embarrassment, as much an instrument of freedom as of limitation.

We could even look around whatever place we happen to be in and count the various gifts history is laying in our laps. The house itself, with the practical details of its construction—walls and roof, plumbing and heat, light and glass. A blanket, a fork, pears and curtains, cookbooks and biography, paper and law, these people.

We were not poured at birth into a concrete block, and if we don't spend time running the fingers of our hearts over these threads that run back to our friends the cephalopods and further, into the eternal silence before the first spark of creation, we will never have the understanding or the enthusiasm to accept "our responsibility towards all those creatures whose agony and groaning have given us birth." [5] And, we might add, whose creative joy, self-expression, and concern for others have made roads for us to walk on and tools to extend them with.

Yes, we can be told, and we would do well to listen and be grateful, take hold and follow. The word "tradition" can have unpleasant connotations, but if we cultivate this friendship with years which have prepared for us roads, roofs, food, warmth and wisdom, whose individuality has melted into our own ability to reason and read and speak, we will feel more at ease with what got here before us. We could even establish a

[5]Nicholl.

mental habit of slipping often during the day into this atmosphere of contact and gratitude. It might dissipate some of our
distrust, some of our anger at having to live with the less
agreeable consequences of history. Most of all, it will make
available to us some of what we need to know in our search for
the meaning of our part in it.

Some, but not all. For learning itself is a wonderfully
slippery business. And learning anything so vast, complex, and
emotionally permeating as one's own person and destiny is the
most extensive exercise of learning that we can undertake. It is
not like memorizing the multiplication tables, or even the
catechism. If our birth did not pour us in concrete, neither did
it fling us out into the wide places the psalmist cries after. The
effort to learn what we are, as the effort to be good, can be a
most unsatisfying necessity. And when the two efforts have to
penetrate each other, our dissatisfaction can become
monumental.

We have all read somebody's autobiographical account of a
religious background, of what—with good intentions all
around—got in and is still in, still causing confusion and pain.
We have cringed at least a little, because what entered the
brain and nervous system of this victim of education is so
manifestly distorted, and because we recognize in those distortions something like our own. If learning enables us to climb
onto someone else's shoulders, it also invites us to sink into
someone else's swamp.

Truth is not an object in a box to which we can be given a
key, especially not the truth about ourselves. Truth, however
reliable the form in which it approaches us, has to filter in

through windows whose glass has been crazed and smeared by all those years of history, and by something else as well—the diffuse and often painful experience of our attempts to find a place in it.

FINGERPRINTS

How deeply we are cherished.
As the price of redemption,
  God gave his son.
As the document of adoption,
  he gives his Spirit.
As the inheritance of those he has adopted,
  he stores up the fullness of himself.
Oh God,
  you lavish yourself on man
  far beyond his dreams.[6]

This is true, and it is beautiful. Some people might acknowledge its truth but not its beauty, for truth can sit gently on the mind and heavy on the emotions. Each of us has a personal image of God which is unhinged from reality in its own individual way. Some of these images have only a few peculiarities, personality flaws which can be endearing. Some make good monsters, and the rest fit somewhere in between.

[6]This is a paraphrase of a passage from the first Pentecost sermon of Guerric of Igny. An English translation of the sermons is available: Guerric of Igny, *Liturgical Sermons*, two vol. (Cistercian Publications, Kalamazoo MI, 1971).

We don't need here a chart of elements which contribute to a disordered religious outlook. These can be found in psychology texts. And I don't want to suggest methods to reform religious instruction in view of better relations with God. I want to speak to people to whom the damage has already been done or is in the unavoidable process of being done. These are the people for whom God has always been a problem; or for whom he seems to have become one in the process of a spiritual life; or for whom the suffering in which they have turned to him for strength and comfort has raised a psychological barrier to the possibility of the very relationship they need in order to bear the suffering.

I want only to glance lightly at a few of the fingerprints on our mental windowpanes, so as not to throw all the blame on problems of self-establishment. There are other factors at work; they too are part of what was waiting for us when we got here, present either in other people or in ourselves—in our nature or in our defects.

Pain

One obvious trouble with God is that he is hidden from the faculties that create our emotional world. We see and hear him indirectly, as one would receive a letter "courtesy of Mr. Jones." And the courtesy which carries his presence is at times questionable. This is compounded by our instinctive sense of God's accountability. Yes, *his.* Our mental landscape is littered with the hurt, anger, and fear which life's events have pressed out of our hearts. Our pain squats down in front of God and says—or would like to say if it dared—"It's your fault."

What life does to us and the interior resources with which we absorb its pleasures and assaults largely determine our emotional attitude toward God. I'm not talking about our moral attitude. The will is the moral force; the understanding gives direction to the will. It can even contribute to the rectification of an emotional imbalance. But the morality of our choices does not necessarily coincide with the emotional effect a situation is having on our experience of God. We can know the right answers and make the right choices and still be thickening the emotional climate in which we experience God. The problem is that we find it difficult to pursue a moral life under such a heavy load of emotion; often the moral effort gets pulled under by emotional forces we do not recognize or understand. We will later look at instances where the moral effort has unknowingly become the servant of the emotion, but the point now is that hurt can build a mountain of rusty nails that sits in the road and calls itself God.

Some people can find the real God through or at least in spite of an experience of pain. For others, the process of suffering is more complex. They cannot carry hurt with the degree of composure they think is proper. So to the pain, they add anger at having to bear it, and anguish at bearing it badly.

For God is not only the sender of circumstance but the measurer of response. And no matter how constructive our religious training has been or how cheerful our natural disposition, we know this. We are accountable to *him*. It's easy to blame the instruction. Truly, it can be disastrous; it can be worse than that because of some previous damage on which it goes to work. But inadequate passing-on of truth is something we can count on having around. History won't unwind itself for our convenience.

I revere St. Therese. I have read all the primary material and go back to it periodically. Yet I know I was harmed by this interest when I was too young to evaluate correctly the place of suffering in her life and mentality. Saints' lives can have awful effects. I can hardly bear to think of St. Alphonsus' terrible vocation, and although I love St. Bernadette, the "I do not promise to make you happy in this life but in the next," the rotting bones, the asthma and the misunderstandings still trigger reactions in me which I know are not healthful. It is an irony that sometimes the people who love God best assist in bestowing on us an impression of God which we ourselves can't love.

This is even more unfortunate because real-life, un-boxed saints are very satisfying epiphanies. Cardinal Medeiros was a fine organizer; he managed to retire our massive archdiocesan debt, and drove himself to death in the shortest term of any Boston ordinary. Yet I always thought he was brought here primarily as a disclosure of the warmth, tenderness, and humor of a God whom our physical eyes see always at second hand. This man could never be put on paper; words don't hold him. Yet those who knew him know God more clearly because of this man who was humble, a gentleman of wondrous involvement in the needs of individuals, and so witty that you laughed yourself to tears at the self-deprecating artistry of his funny stories.

God gives us the real thing so that we will not always be trapped in our hagiography. He gives us the transparent person in compensation for the smudges on the window. But the efficacy of this maneuver is not always as helpful as it might be. The grease on the pane is pretty resistant.

Pleasure

We could use some corrective for our destructive attitudes toward pleasure—the guilt that sends us off in mental corners to enjoy them before God knows we have them and messes them up, or before we ourselves can poison them by feeling that we are less spiritual for having liked them. But we can't blame this tendency wholly on the catechist. For something deep inside us knows that self-discipline is necessary if we are to be decent human beings, if we are to make it possible for others to get along with us. We know that this involves a degree of restraint, the holding in of our tendency to barge ahead and get what we want without order or reflection.

What an impossible road the religious instructor is expected to construct. If we must be spared the saint who lurches into heaven on a path of broken glass, we are no better served by a catechesis of exclusive good cheer. Life has problems; growth is not always comfortable. Comfort is not our birthright and happiness is a hybrid, some of whose genetic contributors are stern and distressing. We need a religious outlook which can embrace a real world with real frustrations, defeats, and rejections, while encouraging us not to manufacture more of these than necessary. We have to try for a balanced expression of what God is about, but not expect more of it than our limited abilities can produce.

Often we want to blame the catechetical method for deficiencies in other forming influences of life. Providing it has its truth on straight, is providing a God who is divine, an incarnation that's historical, a redemption that works, a future that's eternal, and so forth, I think we're unrealistic to complain. Ideally, instruction reaches out and touches the rest of our experience with understanding hands: "See, pay attention. Here is your God. Here is growth. Your catechesis is as broad as the totality of your experience." But part of what we learn from that experience is that nothing is ideal. One of the main themes of religious instruction has to be this acceptance and collaboration with the partial, the disappointing, and the all messed up. How can it achieve its goal if it keeps trying to convince itself and the rest of us that the perfect catechesis will eliminate the caricatures of God which most of us doodle in the sands of daily life?

These distortions bother us because we know or sense or have been told that our search is a double search, and we cannot find ourselves without also finding God. Therefore this crude imitation of what God must be induces a panic. Our search has run out in a mudhole, if this is all it comes to. There's something irretrievably wrong with the equipment. We've learned the truth and it has betrayed us. Other people love God. What's the matter with us?

But perhaps our distortions serve a purpose, one we can't yet recognize. Sometimes we get a glimpse, something more real than either the doctrine we have stored in the brain's filing system, or the defaced icons on the walls of our emotional hallways. Sometimes we suspect that if we could see to the bottom of ourselves there would be a lot more down there than us. God? The real God?

What we tend to forget, because things-being-wrong are so annoying, is that the confusion, the projections, the wounds of destructive religious education or painful life experience are not misfortunes which must obstruct our vision and baffle our search, but gifts of their own kind to help us look. We can blame everything under the sun for conditions we are sure will knock us out of possibility, when these are the conditions which create the possibility in the first place. It is possible that a wizened and disagreeable image of God can be one of these beneficent conditions whose true character we do not recognize.

If God has not thrown off the garments we have woven for him from perverted notions of suffering, pleasure, responsibility, perhaps he has a reason, and perhaps the reason is part of the search.

BUILDING

I like to pray with pictures. One day while rooting in the Common Box, I found a postcard of San Xavier del Bac, and spent several periods of prayer enjoying the remarkable presence of this church. Then I began to wonder what a building like this was doing in the desert. We have grown accustomed to the marriage of Southwestern Indian culture with Spanish Baroque. Accommodations were gracefully made; the mission buildings look as if they had grown there.

But this was so big, so lavish. Here in dusty glory stood a church that was, with all its accommodations, an outcropping of European culture. Was it built for Indians, whose own culture had no acquaintance with the several streams which had fed European Baroque? It was true that this building had not the intrusive character of colonial imposition. It matched. If it didn't seem to have grown there, it seemed to have settled with exquisite grace in a setting which millions of years had been forming to receive it. The book I later found described it this way:

> Two hundred years ago there appeared at Bac a church of
> unearthly beauty. Framed in the warm browns of the surround-
> ing hills and the violet shadows of more distant mountains, San
> Xavier del Bac arises brilliantly white from the desert floor of
> dusty green mesquite and sage.[7]

"There appeared at Bac a church of unearthly beauty . . ."
Not "Padre Velderrain *built* . . .," but "there *appeared*." The
church is called "The White Dove of the Desert," and this too
suggests its evocation of something too beautiful to have been
made. It happened.

Yet it *was* built, by a vigorous friar, his Indian converts,
and—probably—Mexican artisans brought in to complete its
elaborate interior. And it was not built for Spanish settlers, but
for the mission, for Indians who could not possibly trace its
architectural antecedents and who did not need its propor-
tions or its sophistication. Why?

> The reason for this ornate church at this last outpost of the
> frontier is not only to congregate Christian Pimas of the San
> Xavier village, but also to attract by its sheer beauty the
> unconverted Papagos and Gila Pimas beyond the frontier. I have
> thought it worthwhile to describe it in such detail because of the
> wonder that such an elaborate building could be constructed at
> all on this farthest frontier against the Apache.[8]

"Attract by its sheer beauty . . . ." I think there is more to
it than that. Beauty like this does more than attract. It is an
expression of truth which touches not only the mind but the

---

[7]Keiran McCarthy OFM, John P. Shaefer, Celestin Chinn OFM, *Bac* (1977).

[8]Report of Captain Jose Zuniga, commandant of the Tucson Presidio, 1804.
Quoted by Keiran McCarthy OFM, in *Bac*.

senses, emotions, memory, nervous system and whatever else we have to offer. No one who was born and lived in the severe splendor of plain and mountain could have been insensitive to visual beauty. No one reared in an Indian culture could have ignored the correspondence between land and structure. Padre Velderrain and the tradition of which he was in several ways an architect, respected the Indian sensitivity to gifts of the eye. He spoke the language of the eye, and through it reached the whole person. The God of Bac is soaring and sublime, but he belongs to the desert. He matches.

This illustrates the more graceful aspect of our learning process and has its tragic counterpart. We hear not only with our ears but with our whole being, and what we hear is always more than the content of whatever words are used—much more. We understand not only with our minds but with our whole being, and what is created within us is both more and less than the truth.

Consider also that the people who convey truth to us are in the same position. They too have received it through a dense emotional atmosphere and a temperamental inclination which can carry it or betray it with about equal effectiveness. They, as well as we, are immersed in the sensitivities of symbol, image, and sense. The words in which they pass it on may be exact, but words say more than they intend to. Distortion is contagious. We catch it without knowing we are exposed.

To this we have to add that moral, philosophical, and religious instruction is only a fraction of the way in which we learn about ourselves, our destiny, and our responsibility. We begin to learn before we are born. And as soon as we leave the womb we are learning from the touches, voices, reactions of the world we have got into. What we encounter, what is done to us, how our own accomplishments tally with the values we've picked up—all this teaches. It also creates an emotional climate which will receive and affect more formal kinds of instruction. In our daily exchanges with the world, we ask what it is; we want to know what we can expect from it, what it expects from us, what happens when it doesn't give us what we want, how to live with its gifts and disappointments. We touch it, eat it, feel it, hurt from it and enjoy it. We have more control over the weather it raises than a garden does over the sun and rain, but we can't turn off the atmosphere by deciding we don't like it. Control, and the amount of it available to us, are matters of time, balance, and compromise.

Let's consider here more extensively that one element of our interior weather which can have the most serious effects on our reaction to truth: the appreciation we are given of our own worth—more, of our very being.

Some people have received from life such an encouraging sense of their own worth, sometimes of their own superiority, that even an experience of their seamy side will not unbalance them. They can receive expressions of truth with reasonable clarity. They are the ones for whom humility comes most readily. Others have wound up with a sense of self which is unhealably sore.

You cannot always tell the difference from outside. We all know people so aggressive they leave behind a clutter of other people rocking in their wakes. Seasick, you want to scuttle their boats. Tom Dooley had a towering and abrasive fund of aggressiveness, and yet those who knew him well said that it hid an interior self-doubt at least as vast as the confidence he projected.

We would stop in some little village . . . That's when I saw the real Dooley emerge—a shy, lonely man, ridden by doubts and fears, possessed with a burning desire to help but fearful he would be (and he was) misunderstood. And over all this I could see his arching desire to communicate, to let someone else know how he felt. But for some reason. . . Dooley had built a wall around his heart, and this wall was too high for anyone ever to see over it.[9]

Wall-building is an individual enterprise. One person develops an involved, compulsive and idiosyncratic sense of responsibility; another turns into a walking complaint; still another collects important friends. The people who are genuinely at home with themselves may be less competent or more, less ambitious or more, less irritating or more. We can't recognize a wall by its surface. But we do not need here a full list of consequences, still less directions for crippling the sense of worth in ourselves or others. It's one thing we're good at.

We could all say: I am a desire to be someone I can be happy to be, whether or not I think about it much. My natural tendency is to try to get this someone from outside myself, from tangible achievements, from the reactions of others in a variety of relationships. I want success, applause or approval. I strive to surpass or dominate or solidify my place in a group. Conversely, I can become the loner or the master of confrontation. By my argument with it, I use the world to build myself. What we are all doing is reaching out into our environment to pull in some pieces from which to construct a self we can want, a self we can know other people want or at least

[9]Jeff Cheek, in *Before I Sleep*, Ed. James Monahan (Farrar, Strauss and Cudahy, NY, 1961).

acknowledge. This is true whether our experience of ourselves is sturdy or unreliable. Walter Ciszek, SJ, whose story we will be retelling presently, had a secure awareness of himself. He was tough, competent and superior. He stood out into the world and demanded recognition of the person he felt himself to be. But we know other people who carry the self like a small guttering candle, wrapping their hands around it, wrapping their lives around this person they wish were wonderful. Every encounter, every daydream is a drop of oil to feed the illusion that they really are what they want to be.

Perhaps we could say that we start out on our journey, not as one person but three—the first is what we really are; the second is what we feel ourselves to be; and the third is the person we are making, either to compensate for the self we feel is not worth the fuss of living, or—if we are happy to be what we feel we are—to establish this person in the world. An animal will fight hard to maintain its life. We do too.

I am going to keep on assuming that in the wisdom we have been absorbing from our acquaintance with tradition, or in some combination of need and logic, we have recognized that the search for oneself involves the search for God—or at least that we are receptive to this possibility. The person whose sense of self reassures him of the worth of his own existence will have to deal with one less dynamism churning out a distorted impression of God. But although the confident person may relate to God with a fair amount of ease, even his image of God is not entirely accurate. His very confidence can do a job on the truth, as we will see with Fr. Ciszek.

The deformed sense of self will almost certainly stand

midwife to the birth of a nightmare. This thing that we are not creates an emotional projection which we call God, and which sits immobile at every turning of the path—a threat, an object of indifference, or sometimes a succession of horrors so unacceptable we have never dared name them to ourselves. The bruised, deficient self we feel ourselves to be is not the only maker of this thing that never was and whose invasive character we ignore, escape, or fight; but it has a strong hand in the construction of its disagreeable presence.

How ironic that two beings which have no existence can so shape our life. We can be locked into a struggle with the person we are not and the shade of a God who never could be, without even realizing that the struggle exists and that our antagonists do not.

There is more to be said, but before following out this thought, I am going to draw out a little more fully some of the implications of our attitudes toward pleasure. Interest is part of pleasure, and we can be as surely turned from a God who bores us as from a God who magnifies our sense of insecurity. In the development of the spiritual life, the fear of boredom may come first. I am thinking of the comment made by a friend about her son: "I think he is afraid to give himself to God because he feels that if he does, he won't have any more fun."

BOREDOM (I)

God is not a bore. We know this, or at least we know he shouldn't be. Someone whose personality is going to determine the rest of our lives must not be a hood thrown over our heads. And yet many of us have no use for God because he is not interesting, because almost any kind of entertainment is more attractive than he.

What is boredom? We can't help feeling that it is rather an imposition than a negation. It is not just the absence of attraction and interest, but a form of suffering, a positive assault upon our need to love the world, experience it as good. Boredom is not so much absence of delight as the experience of being erased from an exchange of life. Small wonder we dread the duties that lay it on us. Who would willingly approach the slow erosion of his need for being? Boredom is a waste of time, a waste of me.

What do you do then when faced with a God who, you are certain, is bound to wreck your entertainment projects? The word "search" evokes a sense of interest; but what if its goal is the frustration of every urge to enjoy the interesting? We wonder if "danger" is the right word, for danger does not lie heavy on the chest; it chews the stomach. Yet we are in as much danger of boredom as of any other source of pain. It would be no joke to be trapped forever in the withdrawal of everything in which our faculties were made to exercise themselves.

What will happen if we give ourselves to a God we cannot control, who wants in fact to control *us;* if we get really serious about prayer and the responsibilities we anticipate being reminded of by prayer? Will he leave us any fun? Are prayer, reflection, and—worst of all—self-surrender just a lot of holes he is shooting in our lives through which its only enjoyable experiences will ooze away? This is something to think about. Maybe God could wait. There's so much going on, so much he could spoil. "Not now, God. Later. You'll get your share, don't shove." He has other things to do; he ought to be able to let us finish this project, conduct this relationship, succeed in this venture before he sits on our candle for the rest of our lives.

Then of course, he might resent the enjoyment we're getting out of this period of respite, and butt in later with even greater enthusiasm. One never knows what is on his mind. He rumbles on the back burner, his flame just alight, threatening to boil over when he would be most a nuisance. It would seem then that the back burner or the back shed are unsatisfactory solutions to the problem of boredom.

For boredom itself can be less unpleasant than the fear of it, and the diversions in which we try to escape it can often be themselves concealed forms of what we are trying to escape.

Enjoyment

As a form of suffering, boredom can be mild or intense. It has a number of variants, for we are not always bored in the same way or from the same cause. Nor do we always recognize the disease when we have it.

We may be bored with God because, although we don't admit or even know it, we are bored with everything else. We have lost or never had a capacity for enjoyment. Because our faculties cannot find rest in experiences of genuine pleasure, they jump from one pinpoint of excitement to another. Excitement can be a component (or a destroyer) of pleasure, but it is not itself pleasure, and if it becomes our only escape-hatch from boredom, God is hopeless. We will only like him when he makes bubbles to tickle our noses.

> 'I find ecstasy in living; the mere sense of living is joy enough.' When I asked her if she never felt any want of employment, not going off the grounds and rarely seeing a visitor, she answered, 'I never thought of conceiving that I could ever have the slightest approach to such a want in all future time'; and then added after a pause, 'I feel that I have not expressed myself strongly enough.' [10]

And this from someone who suffered much, but not from boredom. Have we lost the capacity to enjoy, to read, to think? Perhaps we don't know it because our environment provides us with enough stimulation to disguise the fact that even the stimulation is a bore. We have lost or never learned the craft of living in an interesting world.

[10]Dickinson. This is from T. W. Higginson's description of his meeting with Emily.

A missioner speaks of pre-evangelization. Maybe we need some of our own. The missioner has a long and patient task—cultivating in an existing culture and religious tradition the soil in which to plant a knowledge of Christ. Much the same could be said of our own personal conversion. Except that there is often no soil to work at in the first place. We need re-education, an asceticism in which our senses are re-trained to be themselves.

It is wrong to view asceticism as the sacrifice of pleasure. Often it can be education to a capacity for pleasure. Enjoying the enjoyable is a virtue; often, not to enjoy it is a vice. Many of us are so incompetent at being pleased that we don't have enough genuine, simple pleasure in our lives to sacrifice if we wanted to. What we have is a superficial substitute. Pleasure is God's creation, and he likes it to be appreciated.

Pleasure gets us into trouble when it steals the place in our hierarchy of choice which other goals should have. When love, service, responsibility retain their place as goals, pleasure tags along—if we know how to create and receive it. Pleasure isn't wrong; putting it in the wrong place is wrong. Pleasure is meant to be harmonized with goals worthy of our nature, and that's what morality is about.

Often this asceticism will lead our capacity for pleasure from one level to another. In this sense it is a sacrifice. Any growth involves some loss for the sake of a greater gain. Our tastes need re-education.

This can happen in many ways. The taste for natural beauty does not always survive a loud, urbanized culture. We can, for instance, begin by listening to soft sound and even to silence. If we've always liked our music loud and with a heavy beat, the process will involve a giving-up, an openness to what does not yet appeal, an act of faith in the power of time. We can be trained to find pleasure in subtle or intricate rhythm, and after awhile we may find to our own surprise that our need for a primitive beat has evaporated. We didn't give it up; it left while we were concentrating on the emergence of a new taste.

We can make up simple programs for ourselves or our group through which new capacities for receiving the beauty of the world can be developed. No big psychological operation is needed. For instance, we can begin to appreciate weather in all its forms.

> 'That's why Camilla and I got married,' Denniston said to Jane as they drove off. 'We both like weather. Not this or that kind of weather, but just Weather. It's a useful taste if one lives in England. Everyone begins as a child by liking weather. You learn the art of disliking it as you grow up.' [11]

We could even ask ourselves if we've ever learned to read, to savor a book of real worth, perhaps to find out why it's so good. It is possible to blow ourselves into glass cocoons. Tense, preoccupied, busy, we use our senses as we'd overdrive a car, abusing, racing, stripping the gears. It's wrong to treat them so unfairly.

Narcisco Irala, SJ, has written a kind of handbook in which he presents one man's appreciation of the part played by the correct use of the senses in a balanced emotional life. He knew because he had used his simple methods to recover from a breakdown.[12] The spiritual writer Agnes Sanford, also once

[11]C.S. Lewis, *That Hideous Strength* (MacMillan, NY, 1946).

[12]Narcisco Irala, *Achieving Peace of Heart* (Joseph F. Wagner, NY, 1954).

the victim of depressive illness, expresses gratitude for the healing help of natural beauty. If learning involves loss, it also involves a gain which will outbalance anything we have to dump along the way.

I would also suggest that one of the principal creators of pleasure is time—elbow room. If we dash from one pleasure to another, none has a chance to grow in us. None has time to lead us into its own particular mystery where we will find out more about our journey and ourselves. Montessori children learn about silence by playing a silence game. They spend time listening to it, until it becomes both a pleasure and more than a pleasure—a place in which to become more than they were. Even people who have problems with time need pleasure, and partial solutions are better than none. Let one interest instead of three sink into the small amount of time available.

I have called this a form of re-education, a rectification of our use of the senses. But it is holy in itself, for God does not wait until we have a good system going. He comes in with the light, the weather, the geraniums; mostly he comes in with the good thing we are creating in letting our faculties reach after their natural balance.

BOREDOM (II)

If there were only one species of boredom, we could dig God out of that hole without much trouble. If re-education of the senses were the only ascesis for which we'd be asked, we could overbalance our catechesis with formation to enjoyment and not have anything to worry about. But another form of boredom concerns the formal spiritual disciplines. If you dangle pleasure over these as an incentive, I'll bite your fingers. Suppose you entice somebody with promises, and prayer turns out not nearly so nice as what one wanted to do instead. Think also of the disagreeable people we have to accept and mind and be patient with if we take the whole thing seriously. This is not a matter of enjoying the green grass. Our world is not an impressionist painting.

Perhaps, since the spiritual disciplines have a unique place in the pattern of life, they ought to have their own word. If the word "pleasure" doesn't fit, something else might—except that nothing seems to, which is just as well. They do not scare me now; they are friends of mine, and elsewhere I have given a slap-dash account of them which shouldn't scare anyone else either.[13] They can often be their own kind of fun. But there is a

[13]Miriam Pollard. *The Laughter of God* (Michael Glazier, Wilmington, DE, 1986).

bogging-down point at which we do a lot of growing up. We have to come to this point in our journey; it is a necessary place to stop, this clearing in the woods, this place of no name. Has anyone, I wonder, ever sat down here and written a prayer to the God of Boredom? It should be done. This unsatisfying clearing is a holy place.

There are several ways of understanding it, and the first is the simplest. It is this: Prayer, the effort to be a better person, the disciplines of spiritual study and reading are also, to a certain extent, acquired tastes. The capacity for living in a Godward direction when the other direction offers a number of compelling attractions is an acquired taste. None of this needs to be awful. None of it needs to be worse than the normal sacrifices we expect to make in the course of a career, a marriage, a faithful friendship. And much of what we consider the spiritual demands of life overlap the demands of our ordinary responsibilities.

We do have to walk off a few cliffs and bear some distressing hours, but we get to prefer the character given to life by prayer and its accompanying disciplines. There is a toughness to the teeth that convinces the teeth they were made for something. I used to like snow pudding as a child. It's made mostly from beaten egg whites and has a custard sauce. I would still like it, but bread and broccoli have their advantages.

The wrong way to tackle the project is to keep asking, "Do I like this? Is my taste improving? Am I increasing my capacity?" You get on with it and leave the rest to God. But you do acquire the sense that this is right, as your life without it would not be. You are being given something deeper than pleasure, certainly—a way of being, a way of pursuing the search for the value of your life, of being more helpful to the world around you. This need not load you up with a sense of gloomy responsibility. Good cheer is not all of virtue, but it is a lot of it, and a gift of it. The sense—even though it comes and goes—of being on the right track is more rewarding than the vague discomfort which comes of wasting our destiny on trifles.

Another explanation comes in the form of questions: What is life for anyway? And what is pleasure? I have seen a delightful letter from a young girl who says that her college years are for having fun; the heavy years will come later. But if you look more closely, you will see what she conceives as fun:

> This semester is even better than last because I know so many more people. It was the best feeling to go to classes and *know* people in them!
>
> I like syllabuses (??) because I know exactly how much work I have this semester. Yes, by May 10th I'll have read 43 books, 20 papers, plus misc. textbooks, reserve reading, etc . . . I really like all my classes—European History, French, Fresh English, & the Modern Novel. Art History is fine. It's a huge class, but I'm learning things I want to know about.
>
> Social life has been better this semester too. It's so nice to meet friends of friends, not people that you wonder if you'll ever run into again. We have a lot of friends who live in East campus—a highrise w/ great views. I love to sit in windows up there and look at the view.

I think she can spend her life having fun, with tastes like that. (The number of books gives me indigestion, but I know college has to force-feed you.) She will probably be the kind of person who can have fun—and make it for others—even under the loads and tragedies of life. I don't know if she has a formal prayer life; I would like her to, for she would be at home in it, and the pleasure she gets out of life would be intensified. I feel sorry for people who do not pray, because they do not live richly enough. The disciplines not only provide a degree of equipment for dealing with inevitable knocks of one kind or another, they heighten the normal beauties of existence. In fact they find some of these in very unlikely places.

Another question is raised by every newspaper, every newscast, every taut and empty face we see: Can I, *may* I dispose of my life according to the standard of whether or not I expect something to be pleasant? Am I greater than the pleasure I seek, and if I am, should I let myself be harnessed to something less than I? Maybe. But just down the road, the needs of my Kampuchean brothers and sisters for privacy, food, blankets, work, and future are asking to be met. I know about other human knots that nobody's fingers seem capable of opening. I know there is too much wrong.

Then can I look at the tools my search requires and say, "No, I'm not interested. They aren't as much fun as a few other things I have in mind." I would say that "not as much fun" is probably wrong; life will undoubtedly grow sharper in the light of prayer. But facing the prospect of sacrifice, do I really have to hesitate over my choice?

At the beginning, we may have to be reassured of the connection between prayer and our value to the world. We may have to be told that the spiritual disciplines will turn out a better person, a better mender of small breaches, a better companion for the rest of the people on the road—even a better force, if distant and unnoticed, for good in South Africa. Being told is part of the beginning. Later we know. We've been through it and we know.

I've read articles by psychologists who are treating people for the psychological damage done by living according to self-centered values. These people are trapped, not in a store-front shelter in East Providence, but in the upward-moving dynamism of an interesting career. They hate the scramble, but they are being created by the sense of their place in it. The psychologists prescribe as therapy some type of unselfishness. It eases the strain to give away some of one's professional skill to people who can't pay for it.

Enclosed beings like this would probably be horrified at the thought of my life, but I could wish them the beauty of a prayer life they cannot see, and the bald spot in the woods that leads to something they don't yet want but will spend forever enjoying.

The third explanation is hardest to grasp. The other two make sense. The third can't. That's its whole point.

> Our gaze is submarine, our eyes
>   look upward
> And see the light that fractures
>   through unquiet waters.[14]

[14]Eliot. Choruses from the *Rock*.

There is a boredom which after awhile, is more interesting than absorption, a mental helplessness which is more right than fascination. The spare space in the trees is necessary because what we are looking for is of a different order than a taste we don't yet have. It is more radically beyond us than that. Once we have been through the bare spot and beyond, simplicity has developed an attraction greater than the intoxication we thought we couldn't give up. "The barely prayable prayer of the bone on the beach"[15]may not be everybody's steady diet, but it is, when we now and then encounter it, if not entertaining , at least extremely real. Even the boredom develops eventually a restful and homely quality we become reluctant to sacrifice.

And perhaps the rightness of all this grows out of the nature of the search. I am more than I think I am, more than I can create for myself. The search is many things—a journey, a vigil, a well, a struggle, a night, a mountain, a city street, a dead end, a door, a swamp and a clearing, a forest and a prairie. I do not want to romanticise what rarely feels romantic, or to dramatise what usually seems more like greasing off the make-up after the footlights go out.

But if you were blind, you—obviously—couldn't see. This makes another kind of sense. If what we are is something we have not yet the ability to see, we have to expect that at least sometimes the process of developing sight is going to show us that we cannot use the sight we don't yet have. It's logical. The terrible thing is not the want of entertainment, but contentment with the lesser form of sight. We might as well get on with it. I won't pretend our disciplines won't sometimes ask

[15]Eliot. *Four Quartets.*

for sacrifice. But in addition to making the unfairnesses of life far more acceptable to us, these almost inconsequential inconveniences are a form of surgery on eyes that often seem determined not to let themselves be opened, convinced that they know all there is to see, and in consequence, limiting the world and their own being to nothing more than they expect them to be.

WAKING IN THE DARK

We could be forgiven sometimes for wondering whether our eyes are getting worse instead of better. When I was young in the monastery, I used to wish that now and then at least, I could get up in daylight. I grew out of it, for if it happened now, I would think the day had gone off without me. I have to wake up in the dark. Spiritually, this is just as true, for the dark is where we are, and we have to see it. Our problem has been the manufacture of a false light. Once we have seen the dark, we can begin to see *in* it, and then we will grow capable of receiving genuine light. This process can also be called self-knowledge.

But what is there to see? What lives in the darkness to which we will awake?

Oneself, first of all. I have said that all of us are three: a real self, a felt self, and a self we are always concocting. God is there too, and those imitations of him we have constructed for ourselves. Previous chapters have reflected on a few of the forces which contribute to their creation—our attitudes toward pain and pleasure; and the effect given to religious instruction by the cultural and emotional atmosphere in which it must be conveyed. Now I would like to look more closely at the effects of a deficient sense of self upon our reception of the truth about God.

It is important, first of all, to realize that the feeling we have about ourselves is not self-knowledge. A poor sense of self is not an awakening. Feelings of inadequacy, guilt, unattractiveness, incapacity can form an emotional pattern which is not conversion, self-knowledge, or anything of the kind. It could be considered a mechanism, a piece of psychic machinery. The person who feels awful about being awkward, hopeless at relation or conversation, intellectually inferior, homely, deserving of dislike, is not necessarily any of these things. Just as the person confident of charm and ability need not be seeing accurately through the lenses of that confidence. But though what we feel about ourselves is not yet knowledge of ourselves, a realization of what this feeling does to us is part of self-knowledge.

For the importance of such a mechanism lies in this, that though it need not reflect the person we are, it can contribute much toward creating in us the qualities we seem to see there, or others that react against them. And as we have noticed, it is also assisting in the production of a distorted view of God.

I think everyone has some relation to God. A negation is some kind of relation. People who relate negatively to God might be grouped roughly into those for whom he is an obstacle to something else they want, those for whom he is intellectually difficult, and those whose distorted image of him is impossible to accept. These basic attitudes can produce a number of combinations and variations.

But many also are the complicated attitudes of people who have retained some kind of bond with a church or have taken a very personal interest in God. Some retain the bond only because they do not feel free to get away; some are genuinely bewildered at why the whole thing has turned out so badly.

The God of the Wounded Self

First, an aching sense of self can make an illusory God who feels about us as we expect to be felt about. If we feel uninteresting, he will not be interested. If we feel weak and self-centered, he will be mad at us. This is a fairly straightforward expectation. But it is in the area of moral effort that emotional complications multiply. By moral effort I mean response to the legitimate demands of our nature, demands which have been expressed in what we call—sometimes without much sympathy—conventional moral standards.

I have spoken before of our sense of accountability to God. This is a fundamental element in our apprehension of God. We don't make it. But what happens to it emotionally can depend heavily on our way of experiencing ourselves. The felt self does not invent moral responsibility, but it can remake it into the nightmare it was never meant to be.

This does not mean that we are better off being bad, or erasing the distinction between good and bad. If being good can be a delicate and occasionally dangerous business, being bad is more dangerous and less delicate. Everyone thinks of sex when you say "morality." That's only one aspect, but it has a place. I remember a column by Dolores Curran, who works extensively in the field of family relations. She detailed not only the suffering but also the personality damage got into by some of her young friends who had tried live-in arrangements. A friend who teaches in college tells me that he sees young people hardening to ward off the pain of these temporary encounters, and I have friends of my own whose experience of life became more painful than it had to be when they forgot that morality is only our nature asking not to be hurt.

But sexual morality is not the whole story. Justice has many faces, some of which are far too easy to veil. Honesty is a moral challenge; patience; respect for the differences of race, religion, and political persuasion which knock on the doors of our understanding in every person we meet.

There are people for whom the big elements of morality are not hard, or not usually hard, and the people who could easily do much better with a few precautions and some effort. For the latter, what I have called the disciplines will open a new world of interest and enrich their attitudes toward moral effort.

For others the big things are and always will be a problem. They live on the brink, not just occasionally, but all the time. They fall over and climb back, even though they often feel it isn't worth the effort. Why not just drown and get it over with? But the effort is worth it. And prayer is worth it even when one has taken the latest nose-dive and feels that the last thing in the world one wants to confront is God.

For these people, life is a scramble for moral handholds, a going under and a crawling back just one more time—and then another one more time, while people for whom basic morality is not so hard go about their charities. Prayer can be one more heroic act in a series of heroic acts by which they keep refusing—just one more time—to give up the struggle. People who are on the brink or over should pray and read and keep learning about God. They should make efforts at the things which are easier, even when they feel that, right now, the big thing is impossible. Not because the big thing doesn't matter, but because moral accomplishments, even on a smaller scale, make them and their world much better. And who knows? The small triumphs might lead a path to the big one. God has beautiful ways of showing appreciation for this type of struggle.

Whatever our capacity for responding to them, a poor sense of self will affect our emotional attitude toward the demands of moral effort. This can be especially so as the effort becomes more refined. Some men find it easy to remain faithful to their wives, but difficult to think gently of the guys who walked over their heads to promotion.

People who feel inadequate, no matter what their objective moral accomplishments, will live with a God of demands that can never be met—the relationship with God seems to require a person we are convinced we can never be. It's like being caught in a game whose stakes are life and death, when we not only hold all the losing cards but *are* in some way the losing hand.

To make it worse, this kind of person often feels compelled to be perfect, God or no God. Perfection is felt to be the only way of becoming someone worthy of love and capable of success. So we project this compulsive need for perfection onto the God of morality. *He* must expect what *we* feel it necessary to provide. And if we can't do it, he is to blame; he is asking for what he has not equipped us to give. The possibility that he might be understanding or even put our failings to some good use never occurs to us—at least on an emotional level.

The most comforting doctrines can get crushed in the gears and hang around, unrecognizable, in our mental darkness. The Redemption is particularly vulnerable. There are people for whom the Passion of Christ is not reassurance but accusation. They face the shreds of this dying man with, "I did that to him and I'm not good enough to stop doing it." Any number of projections can shadow the cross. Most of us know people who enjoy suffering from other people and letting them know it—as a way of alleviating some emotional disorder which may or may not have a connection with the pain at hand. Our habitual reaction to this can rise against the Christ who in all innocence has gotten between us and our experience of being this kind of victim.

Or if we are psychologically conditioned to need suffering as a way of expiating real or imagined guilt, we can turn the doctrine of reparation into a quest for pain to relieve the greater suffering of feeling guilty. In this case the difficulties with pleasure and pain which we have already discussed slip into the current of a defective sense of self and are intensified. For we will be uneasy with pleasure and miserable at the pain in which we seek absolution from a guilt our emotions can never escape.

Of the other ways in which the good news of the Redemption can become for us very bad news indeed, I will give only one: If our pain can be used to "save souls", the more pain the better, right? If God wants to save souls, we are sitting ducks. Pain must be the most valuable thing in the world and what we can expect most of. The crucifix says to us, "This is what you're in for."

Not only the Redemption but the entire body of doctrine can be unhinged by the last difficulty I will mention. I put it last because although it can sound somewhat like the one at the head of the list—expectation of rejection—it is really its opposite. God, in this situation, is the one whom we do not want, the one with whom an intimate relationship is distasteful to an absolute degree. But aren't we assured that his relationship to us is precisely this? We will admit he is loving, generous, and considerate, but we would like him to keep his distance. It has nothing to do with his reputation for interference. Interference is not what we dread, but closeness. We wish only that he would go away.

Better balanced people may laugh at the litany of distortion which an afflicted heart levels at the creator and lover of the universe. But this does not make it less accurate an expression of the sufferer's distress. A single phrase of it can touch somebody's wound; and some people—in spite of the laughter—can run down the list checking off one item after another. For them, God is the computer into which a human being is entered and processed, a silence of infinite dissatisfaction. He is what doesn't help when our little triumphs blow a fuse, the dry rot in all the buildings where our emotional investments have been stacked. It is he who leans on our horizons with long elbows, and provides himself as the other side of an equation whose first term is one's own inescapable inadequacy. He is the banker in human pain, counting out payments for his redemptive projects; the intrusive visitor against whom one's stomach tightens as one serves the unavoidable luncheon; the violator of one's secret room. He is the crucified and infinite recrimination.

How melodramatic. Indeed, how impossible. And yet for millions of people God is an unacceptable solution to the question of life. And not all of these find him so because they want something with which he is incompatible. For some, the God of this litany is the only God there is. For some, he is an undercurrent, a slight disturbance on the reliable surface of event. For some perhaps, no trouble at all. But how do those who are, with or without conscious awareness, crippled by their apprehension of God, manage to get on with such a formidable companion?

Getting On: The Wrong Way

Some people obviously don't. Because they know a God like this is impossible, or because some attraction incompatible with God promises to heal their wounds and fill their needs, or because they see no compelling reason to believe God exists— this one or any other—they enter what I have called a negative relationship with him. They cross him off the list of things they consider real.

But we do not have to be atheists to do away with God. Another way is to pretend he's really very nice and we have no trouble with the books. We will be very good, very moral, not out of love for morality or God, but because we can't bear to be anything else. The phantom God our self-doubt has summoned up can be harnessed to the carriage of the kind of self which will impress our world and deny our fear. Our religious activities cascade from the need to feel ourselves good, approved, successfully spiritual. This is what I referred to as the "danger" of being good. We use goodness as a way of escaping from a real relationship with God.

For some, being bad will do as well as being good. Or we can settle for such a spate of interesting activities and reassuring achievements that we need pay no attention to our problem with God. Or one's whole being can be knotted into a fist. We can rebel against moral authority or in the name of moral authority, because the object of the rebellion is the rectification of what we feel we are.

Another possibility is despair. There's so much to get done, so much we resent and bear as badly as possible because hating life is our only way of punishing the God and the people who have inflicted it on us. Practical despair can go to Mass every day, feed its family and collect a salary for efficient labor.

But what of those who found the litany unrealistic and overdone? They felt no chill of recognition. "Oh no," they say, "my God is not like that at all. I've had the most wonderful friendship with God. My God is not too small—too big is all, too beautiful. I don't have time enough to pray as much as I'd like. I want him with all my heart." Good. This also is the room to which you must wake up some night. And you have the most profound and beautiful literature to help you see what's there. The difficulty will be that the descriptions may not sound as if they apply to you; a certain disorientation attends the dark. But we will get to that later.

The person whose sense of worth has been given a solid ground, or who in spite of some admixture of insecurity has been able to wipe the window pane and let reality come in with a minimum of distortion is a gift to the world, a place of reference. These people have lighted the window for others on cold evenings. They witness to the reliability of spiritual tradition.

If you do not fit in the group which has trouble with God or in the group which doesn't, you have lots of company among those whose inner world has something of each—images of God to attract and burden, to desire and run from, as well as a self of pain and one of confidence.

PART TWO
WAKING

THREE WAKE

But the inventory is not exhausted. In fact it has hardly begun. Everything I have detailed is, taken all together, a fly-speck on the rest of what is there. For most of it so far—the felt self, the self I try to be, the fabricated God—is distortion, an elaborate mistake. The rest of what is there is real, and whether we see it or know it, its reality expands and presses so exuberantly against our inner walls, that the puzzle is how our colossal fund of misinformation can find a crack to hide in, let alone extend so effective an influence over our attitudes and choices.

What is there?

I am there, the person I really am, the person whose being fits so perfectly that I need not give myself a thought. God is there, with a character full of pleasant surprises. God and myself, securely situated, wrapped unobtrusively in the mystery of each other.

All the broken pieces of truth which have filtered through the greasy pane are lying about, clues mostly, but each holding the possibility of being helpful. And voices, however scrambled their sentences, struggling to work free of the questionable environment in which our world and our reactions have set them. The voice of Scripture, and news brought by the beauty of nature, by humanity's interpretive accomplishments—the Bacs, the sailing vessels and symphonies, the cooperative ventures that have worked, or at least been tried; voices of people who have not gone down under the load of compensation, ambition and greed; the small, steady rustle of voices warming a darkness we have not learned to explore, or perhaps even to see.

Awakening is not always comfortable, but it's the sure way of getting to all this good stuff, all this reality. By way of illustration, I will draw on the lives of three people. Two have stories and one doesn't. Two have a spiritual life, and one doesn't. Two are fairly unusual, and one is like you and me.

I found one of the stories not long ago in an article on the psychological effects of Vietnam. The experience is real; the name understandably is not. The author refers to this man as Billie Lee.

> Billie Lee's entire life had been duty-bound. "I was a kid who never screwed up ever," he said. "I fought off the drugs at home and in Vietnam because I always wanted to do things just right. When I got wrapped up in my job in the army, I did it so I could come home the same person I was when I went away."[1]

The story of our second awakening is better known. Walter Ciszek, SJ, begins the account of his Russian adventure with, "I think you have to know I was born stubborn. Also I was

[1]John Sangone, "The War That Has No Ending" (*Discover*, June, 1985.) Further texts on Billie are from this article.

tough." The Society of Jesus did not appeal to him because obedience did not. He entered anyway because "since it was so hard, I would do it." I can't say he did it very well, since "without any permission,"

> I continued my practice of going without certain things and of undertaking annoying jobs, just to condition myself to do the harder thing and to strengthen my will. With this in mind, I wrote my thesis "On the Training of the Will."[2]

When he was arrested and sent to Moscow's Lubianka Prison,

> I had a great deal of confidence in myself. I hardly thought the interrogators would get me to admit to something I hadn't done...I felt I could probably hold my own against any interrogator.[3]

The woman without a story I will call Jo. Warm and courageous, she is gifted in appearance, character, and personality. Although her situation is like yours and mine, she is the kind of person of whom her closest friend could say, "I'm not like Jo. I'm not as good as she," and I could think in response, "Very few people are." She has reared a large family with good-humored grit, often so house-bound she was "glad to dump the garbage, just to get out a few minutes."

[2]Walter Ciszek SJ, with Daniel Flaherty SJ, *With God in Russia* (McGraw-Hill, 1964).

[3]Walter Ciszek SJ, with Daniel Flaherty SJ, *He Leadeth Me* (Doubleday, NY, 1973). The remaining texts of Walter Ciszek are quoted from this book.

The experience of waking does not always have a conscious religious dimension. You do not come in for it because you've taken up with God, any more than you can avoid it by keeping him at a safe distance. It could dump itself into the life of someone whose church-going is an irritating formality, or another who has cheerfully assumed his favored status with God. It could happen to someone who does not believe in God, to another for whom God is a serious emotional difficulty, or to still another who has been profoundly attracted by him. It just happens.

Fr. Ciszek had a point of reference in God; in fact, an unusually solid one. He had been living a life of prayer and following a rather bull-headed program of asceticism for several years. Jo also was seriously spiritual. In the teeth of a trying vocation, "I never questioned my friendship with God." The young soldier seems to have lived on a totally secular level, for whatever his church-going program might have been, God has no part to play in his drama or its resolution.

Psychologically, it is possible to be, as Fr. Ciszek seems to have been, an uncomplicated person whose emotional attitude toward himself coincided with the self he put forward to the world. He really felt confident and tough; confidence and self-assertion were not compensatory reactions to a sense of inferiority. He was proud—with reason—of his unbreakable body and the will he had trained to high capacity.

Of Billie's felt-self, I can only guess. It probably had been weakened by his broken home. For whatever reason, he needed to experience himself as good; he worked hard at it. Before Vietnam caved in on him, he was to himself a reliable and decent man, confident in the goodness he had always managed to turn out. He expected to bring home the same goodness he had taken to Vietnam.

Jo thinks ill of herself—not to the point of neurosis; but her beauty, strength, and talent do not erase a deep sense of being less good than most people at everything she would like to be and do.

We are talking now about three people who, once awakened, did not go back to sleep. They couldn't, they had to get up.

> There was only one time when Billie Lee didn't stay wrapped up in his work, when doing his job well collided head-on with his sense of morality. "Our people had rounded up some civilians and accused them of working with the Viet Cong. I knew the civilians. They weren't the enemy. Something was going to happen, and I knew I didn't want to be part of it. So I asked to be taken off duty involving those people. Well, they relieved me, and then someone took the civilians out and killed them all.

Billie kept dreaming of home, sharing his plans with a close friend, counting the days until his discharge date in October. He anticipated the holidays, the football games, and a world with nobody in it to kill. On his last day of service, packed and ready to go, he and his buddy were detailed with a group of South Vietnamese to a trouble spot which turned out to be hotter than his commanding officer had foreseen:

> His unit ran into heavy enemy sniper fire, and several of the South Vietnamese were killed. "Well, they all started to run," Billie Lee said, "and I ran too. The rest is hard for me. It's not easy to admit that you ran when your buddy was hit, and you

knew he was still alive, and you left him because you were so scared and all you could think about was getting out of there and going home to a football game."

Walter Ciszek recalls the erosive effect of long interrogation:

My case entered its 12th month and the interrogations still continued. My patience and my self-confidence, even my innate stubbornness were gradually wearing away.

I gave up, I convinced myself that my efforts were useless and I let the process roll on with a shrug. After all, I said to myself, what does it really matter? What difference can it possibly make to anyone except to me—and I simply wanted out.

His interrogator presented him with a falsified account of his testimony, and when he held back confirmation, broke the crust of his last resistance with a quick threat. Fr. Ciszek signed the fat sheaf of paper, page by page.

It was a moment of agony I'll never forget as long as I live. I was full of fear yet tormented by conscience. After signing the first hundred pages, I stopped even the pretense of reading the rest. I just wanted to finish signing them as quickly as possible and get out of the interrogator's office.

I had yielded, in that one sickening second, to fear, to threats, to the thought of death. When the last page was finished, I literally wanted to run from the interrogator's office.

It was not like that for Jo, as it is not like that for most of us—no alarm clock so penetrating that it threatens to shatter the personality at its foundation. Instead, the soft and slowly increasing buzz of a discomfort which will not go away—an uneasiness, a sense of inevitable failure before one's hand is set to the task.

This sense has not come of being left with an empty house and a deserted ego. Her hours have not turned to echo chambers for the previously unheard footfalls of a natural sense of inadequacy. She is only slightly less busy than she has ever been, but she is faithful to a daily half hour of prayer, and her whole being has been open for years to the common and extraordinary surrenders of friendship, marriage, work, and motherhood. She just grew. "I guess I'm a late bloomer." Not really. God has been fashioning the person who was ready to handle the waking when it came.

She feels that other people have it all together. If someone wrote it down, perhaps she could find a way to fix up her life, come off better with God. Is there something very good to read? She would like precise directions so as not to get mixed up.

Three at the point of waking. It can come in other ways. For the Franciscan troubadour, John Michael Talbot, the end of a disastrous marriage provided the shaking up. This or something else can do the job for anyone. But ordinary alarm clocks will do: any relationship which has bungled an immense hope; the job that was going to unfold one's capacities and disclosed instead only one's greed and indifference to others; a charitable project in which the needy became an enhancement of one's own need for appreciation; the ascetic program that twisted religion like a band-aid around the wound of one's defective self-image.

It's not much fun to wake up, but the question is then what to do with the dark. We've seen it, probably for the first time. This is not the false and soggy feeling about a lousy self; this is what we've actually done or failed to do, a corrupt pattern of behavior to which we have committed ourselves, a weakness

so radical that we cannot perform the good we are called upon
to perform, a dim but inescapable sense of knowing we cannot
measure up.

> One need not be a chamber to be haunted,
> One need not be a house;
> The brain has corridors surpassing
>   material place.
>
> Far safer, of a midnight meeting
>   External ghost,
> Than an interior confronting
>   That whiter host.
>
> Far safer through an Abbey gallop,
>   The stones achase,
> Than, moonless, oneself encounter
>   In lonesome place.
>
> Ourself, behind ourself concealed,
>   Should startle most;
> Assassin, hid in our apartment,
>   Be horror's least.
>
> The prudent carries a revolver,
>   He bolts the door.
> O'erlooking a superior spectre
>   More near.[4]

[4]Dickinson

BILLIE LEE

Hearing the alarm is only a small part of waking. What we do next is more important. Some people tend to lie in the dark, counting its discomforts, multiplying the intensity of its shadows.

This was what Billie did. He could hardly have done more things wrong if he had deliberately set out to handle his pain as badly as possible. He left Vietnam the next day, came home to "a hostile community, to a seven-month-old kid, to a lot of obligations, and with a lot of shame." He had no choice about all this. But he did choose to tell no one about what had happened. He felt there was no one to tell. Telling would create people who knew, whose presence would scrape at his wounded psyche and deepen a humiliation that was now too hard to sustain.

Alone. The isolation of a man like this is hard to imagine. Other people were simply things which must not know. How could he love? No one could love him back, not if they knew. He could not even really give to others, because if they knew, they would repudiate the gift. If he had had a God around,

God would have been someone who knew, a threat to the compromise he was making with the dark, a confirmation of his own self-condemnation.

Whatever his felt-self had been in the beginning, it was terrible now, and it was dominant. He tried to rebuild the person he had taken to the war:

> To forget, to bury his frequent thought of suicide, he plunged into his work, eventually moving up to a responsible position. But the depression was there and the drinking, both of them much worse in the fall. In the first few years, the symptoms were mild. But as time passed, the blues deepened and the boozing increased.

He went to the Vietnam Veteran's Memorial in Washington, because he'd heard it could be "a place of healing, where a vet from Nam could mourn and resolve his nagging guilt." The visit only increased his desolation. Finally, he went to one of the Vet Centers which the VA has set up to assist this kind of problem. He takes part in therapy twice a week, "rap sessions with fellow survivors who had similar experience."

> The groups have helped Vietnam vets deal with their feeling of being used, abused, and discarded . . . They are vital to a vet who still needs the absolution that society denied him when he returned from the war. They've enabled many veterans to forgive themselves.

Let's forget God a minute, since he seems to have played no conscious role in Billie's story. What has happened? The person Billie wanted to be, *had* to be, was destroyed by Vietnam. He tried to put it back together. It was the only kind of self he knew anything about, the only kind he was able to want. "I'd tried so hard all these years, and I was sure I was going to make it right." But the broken pieces tore at his inner flesh. I find it very beautiful that instead of committing suicide he went for help. It took 15 years, but he wound up in a storefront Vet Center. At the price of the secrecy in which he had buried the ruin of himself, he is finding another self to want, or at least to accept. If what you want to be and have tried to be is gone, and you can't get it back, then unless you discover there is something else to be, you will go on as the victim of impossibility and never have much of a say in your own becoming. But you can learn that there is something new to want, and grow to want it. This growth depends on seeing the wreckage of what you tried to be, and letting it be seen—not just seen but handled—by people who are also finding something more real to want. I don't mean the whole wide world, but somebody who can help.

Heroes

Is there anything better than being good, reliable, and heroic? Is there anything better than giving one's life for a friend? I think that is not the point. There is something better than manufacturing the kind of self we feel we have to be; and that is to begin, little by little, to find and become what we really are. If this involves giving one's life for one's friend, or one's enemy, then it is the better thing. But the question is not simple.

Often the particular *way* in which we are being good and even heroic is an extension of our campaign to compensate for feeling worthless, or at least to create a kind of worth which is unreal. The *manner* in which we handle our moral choices can be harmful, even though the choices themselves are correct. We are using what is good in itself to become something we are not. And when the campaign breaks down under the strain, even the effects of a bad moral choice can be drawn up into a moment of waking, and can initiate a movement away from the contrived and into the true. This is what happened to Billie. We would be wrong to court moral evil, but having gotten into it, we would be even more wrong to surrender to despair because we have damaged the self whom we should never have been trying to manufacture in the first place.

We must also consider that some of the greatest acts of heroism are performed in the acceptance of an incapacity for heroism. Some people make perfectly fine heroes. They choose and act according to the good, in spite of fear and repugnance. And even in the successful accomplishment of their project they remember chiefly the fear and the unwillingness. They bring an essential modesty to brilliant deeds. Others are chained to their own brilliance, prisoners of their need for heroism or protest or nonconformity, reaction or moral superiority. The deed succumbs to the display. And still others must practise the heroism of retracing their steps from moral disaster to the fork in the road at which they decided to be someone they are not.

If you think it out, there are roughly three types of good action. First, the kind in which one's sense of worth and importance is enhanced. I assist in a project for the elderly, and from the very gift of my time and ability I am given a degree of self-satisfaction. I am a skilled counselor and donate several evenings a week to a clinic. Both my career and my charity give me a sense of being helpful. Secondly, we have the kind of good which neither enhances nor endangers one's sense of self-esteem. I execute the mechanical aspects of my job without much feeling one way or the other—the typing, the dishes, the computer work are part of a larger endeavor and they capture neither my mind nor my emotions to any extent. Thirdly, there is the kind which erodes one's sense of self. I push another into the limelight I would like to have. I refrain from defending a blunder I am accused of making. I accept my own incapacity for an achievement I long to make; I learn how to live with the memory of having failed, either morally or materially, at an endeavor whose accomplishment was necessary to my conception of myself as worthy of love and admiration.

The person who performs an act of heroism out of a pervading sense of self-display or even of moral compulsion (I can't live with myself if I don't) may well have an obligation in conscience to perform the act anyway. The presence of second-rate emotional components doesn't erase the moral imperative involved. It is right and necessary to try to save the buddy's life, to defend the civilians unjustly suspected. It should be done. But its doing can be, for some people, if they have the luck to bring it off, one more brick in the edifice of a self for display. Eventually, even these heroes have to face an awakening of some kind if they are to become real.

Those who haven't made it, who got scared and ran or who realize that they have other, more subtle habits of running out on moral demands, have the opportunity for another heroism—the good of accepting their own defeat and moving through it onto the right road to themselves, a better relationship with others, and a more genuine morality.

If our job or our charities (which all told are usually more justice than pure benevolence) give satisfaction, we should be grateful. Why not? Satisfaction is natural, necessary, and good. But if we land in unsatisfying situations or if we blow the right to some satisfaction or other, then gratitude is also due. Success, for us at that point, might have dumped us in a swamp of unreality.

The Gift of Shame

What is a person like Billie doing in his therapy sessions? It is interesting that although a professional counselor is present, these sessions are constructed substitutes for the natural therapy which other wars have offered to long-term buddies talking it out on a protracted journey home. Because of its particular set-up, the Vietnam War provided neither long association nor a long return trip. Now the Vietnam vet is getting in his storefront center what other men got in a troop ship and from a tumultuous welcome home. The human race is accepting him again. He can come home to his own heart.

The article relating Billie's story uses the words forgiveness and absolution, ciphers for a reality most of us want but don't well understand. The first thing Billie will find out is that he is not alone. He has lots of company. Others have blown themselves to pieces too. His story doesn't shock them; they are as relieved as he to know they aren't alone. As a matter of fact, the very shame that has been secretly poisoning him is a bond that draws him close to his weak and humiliated fellows. He had worked hard to set up a self that couldn't be disapproved of, and had smashed it all up. Now, people—the outside, the world on which his self-esteem depended—are walking softly over the ruins, and accepting, not the flawless projection he considered deserving of love, but the real person who can be loved whether or not he deserves it.

Isn't this what we would give most to have? The assurance that it is oneself who is of value before and beyond and in spite of whatever we can deliver by way of achievements, constructions, and even moral behavior? The world admires many people whose morality is outstanding—Mother Teresa, Queen Elizabeth, Archbishop Camara, Anne Lindbergh. But is it integrity alone which we admire, or is it not also the warmth and humanity which integrity has nourished in people of this kind? And doesn't this form of goodness, or this manner of being good, grow out of the precise situation we most want—to be assured of our own value independent of the value of our action, and out of this assurance to express by the correct moral choices, our gratitude for the gift of being worthy of love? It's a terrible thing to be chained to the need to make oneself worthy of anything. But the person who knows himself, however dimly in the flickering dark, to be already graced with value can embrace the effort to be good with something like a chance of letting goodness be what it was meant to be—a celebration of the gift of being worthy of love. This person can stop trying to turn his moral effort into one more cog in the machinery of constructing a worthy self.

In Billie's almost totally secular framework, he could be told that goodness is illusory anyway, that his moral lapses and the emotional impact of walking away from the killing of people he knew to be innocent were accidents in a nature whose actions have no moral significance. They were products of a stressful world for which he has no responsibility. I would be sorry if he fell for this, because responsibility is a privilege as well as a road to the self he is beginning to find.

I would not only be sorry if Billie were persuaded that there are no such things as moral standards, I would be surprised. The hell he has enjoyed since Vietnam has convinced him that there are. The point is that morality is not a bag of rocks which we hoist onto our backs. It is the weak and often fractured human personality dealing with greater or less success with a world of inner and outer demands, stresses, outrages, desires, joys, interests, and possibilities. It is a personality whose innate beauty can be counted upon and whose capacities can be drawn out not only by sensible discipline but by the warm and humble acceptance of a failure which gives birth to that other try and another and another.

Forgiveness is an inadequate word. Forgiveness is not the condescension of a guiltless being or a stand-by society toward someone who has violated some or any of a series of strictures. Forgiveness means being given back yourself with your wounds turned into sources of compassion and humble joy. They may never be healed but they become creative rather than destructive. They give to your integrity a quality of suppleness, humility and peace that it otherwise could not have. They do not eat you any more, but that is far from all of it. They turn you outward.

Billie will have discovered that morality is not something to which he has a right by dint of being better than all those other guys who live bad lives. It is a fragile possession, and one whose nature he can see more realistically. He also sees, if shapelessly, the contour of the self he has felt himself to be and how the emotional dynamism it creates has influenced the character of his attitude toward morality and the creation of a substitute personality.

Most important, he has found out a few things about his

real self. He has seen the shadows and acknowledged his responsibility for them, the weakness and the worth of the being he really is. Will this heal him? Probably not. He can realize now that he was in need of healing before he got to Vietnam and that his traumatic war experience has let him see the darkness which was always there. But whether or not he can ever think of himself as healed, he has a chance now of dealing with the injury, of handling both it and the life it confronts. And this with some degree of realism, humor, and humility.

I said at the beginning of this chapter that we were going to set God aside for awhile, since he plays no role in Billie's consciousness. That does not mean he plays no role at all. Circumscribed by a world without God, Billie has no false God to reject or be afflicted by. But he also lacks the rest of the clues to who he is himself. This is about as far as he can go. He has met the spectre in the dark house and seen beyond its horror. Goodness will sit less tensely on his mind. There's a lot more in the dark however, that he will never see in this life. And if he has forgotten God, God has not forgotten him. He is a child of Advent, a man determined by waiting for what he does not expect—the self-disclosure of circumstances which to him have been purely secular, the realization that they have a personal face and a meaning he has never anticipated.

WALTER CISZEK

We can bring God all the way back now, because Fr. Ciszek awoke, not to the absence of God, not even to a fabricated God, but amazingly, to the real thing.

He returned to his cell after signing the account of his interrogation, strangling with shame:

> My will had failed; I had proved to be nowhere near the man I thought I was . . . I was tormented by feelings of defeat, failure, and guilt. Yet above all, I was burning with shame. I shook with spasms of nervous tension and release.

We saw that Billie revealed his shame to no one. Fr. Ciszek, in solitary confinement, had no one to talk to anyway. But, unlike Billie, he was not alone. "When at last I began to regain some control of my nerves, my thoughts, and my emotions," he tells us, "I turned to prayer as best I could." It was a good honest prayer. He dumped on his own head all the abuse he could dig up; then he started in on God. Why had the Spirit abandoned him when he had so needed the right words, the strength and courage to resist his fear? Why at least had God not struck him down with a heart attack before he could so disgrace the Church?

Then he began to wonder at the intensity of his shame. The guilt of his action could not have been great enough to deserve so absolute a reaction—his signature had been wrenched from a man half-mad with fear. That moment's action was disproportionate to his emotional response. Yes, that *moment's* action, but what of the moments and the years which had marched directly up to that moment and in it declared themselves to him?

> I was ashamed because I knew I had tried to do too much on my own and failed. I had asked for God's help, but had really believed in my own ability to avoid evil and meet every challenge.

For years, he had been faithful to prayer.

> Yet I had been thanking God all the while that I was not like the rest of men, that he had given me a good physique, steady nerves, and a strong will, and that with these physical graces given by God, I would continue to do his will to the best of *my* ability.

And what a dull imitation of God he had created in the process—a spectator in the box, a cheerleader, a picture gazing immobile from its hook on the wall. God was the packed house before which he engaged in his chronic competitions, the servant of his projected self, the slightly dangerous dog leashed just out of reach. God was the clay he had kneaded around the armature of his religious practices to construct the man he was determined to be.

> Had I failed to see that these [religious practises] were not always done solely in response to God's grace or out of some apostolic motive but also out of pride? Yes, I prided myself on doing these things better or more often than others.

He had vied with the legends of the saints to show himself and the world that they were no better than he, and that he was a good deal better than the current crop of religious heroes. He had spent his life seeking God's will by identifying it with his own and drowning out the voice of the Spirit with the decibels of his own desires, until under the interrogator's intimidation,

> I was so intent on hearing only one message, the message I wanted to hear, that I was not really listening at all. Whatever else the Spirit might have been telling me in that hour, I could not hear. . . Long ago, I had decided what I expected to hear from the Spirit and when I did not hear precisely *that*, I was betrayed.

I wonder how many of us, from the instruction we got in religion class, would recognize in this experience the making of a saint? Walter Ciszek was an unusual man, not because he achieved great things—as he did—but because almost immediately he was able to accept the devastation of a self at whose construction he had labored all his life. He made peace with his own demolition.

> The Spirit had not abandoned me, for the whole experience had been his work. I had failed miserably to be what I professed to be . . . And yet that moment of failure was in itself a great grace, for it had taught me a great lesson. Severe as the test had been, God had sustained me by the light of his grace.

Wouldn't you think enough would be enough? Now they could cart off to Siberia a man who knew, and had been willing to accept, that his entire service of God and neighbor had been an elaborate exploitation of both for the benefit of a footlight sanctity with his name on the marquee. With the humiliation of Lubianka to temper his arrogance, he could walk gently among the lost and suffering, burying his ambitions in a real and helpful charity.

Not at all. He knew. But knowing wasn't enough. And although Walter Ciszek is unusual in the totality of his response to this experience, the pattern of his growth is not unusual at all. I wouldn't talk about it if it were. Anyone who has awakened to this darkness knows quite well that to see it doesn't guarantee one's ability to walk around in it. You think, "Now I know. Now I see. I surely won't do *that* again. Life will be different now." And it isn't. Knowing you are weak, ambitious, and greedy doesn't make you strong, humble, and unselfish. It only makes it easier to recognize the weakness and self-absorption the next time they take flesh in a choice. Knowing isn't enough.

> It was not enough for me to understand that the experience of Lubianka was designed by God to purge me of dependence upon self and to lead me to reliance only upon him. After the terrible time of the past year and its ultimate crises, I had come at last to understand that truth. But understanding of itself does not lead to practice or accomplishment; and it was to the practice of purgation that I was now led.

In the next four years of cat-and-mouse with interrogators who were trying to coerce his collaboration with the NKVD, Fr. Ciszek never lost his fear—fear not of them but of himself.

"Having failed once, I was literally terrified that I might fail completely this time and lose the last thing I still clung to, my faith in God." He wasn't wrong.

> It was not the Soviet government versus Walter Ciszek. It was God versus Walter Ciszek...The primacy of the self that had manifested itself and been reinforcing itself even in my methods of prayer and spiritual exercises underwent a purging that left me cleaned to the very bone.
>
> Every time I brought myself to the point of calling a halt to the proceedings, of taking some firm stand, I faced again that awful moment of decision and of weakness—and finally of indecision. I could not do it.

Until he woke to a darkness he had never imagined possible:

> One day the blackness closed in around me completely. Perhaps it was brought on by exhaustion, but I reached a point of despair... I knew I was approaching the end of my ability to postpone a decision... I saw only my own weakness and helplessness to choose either position open to me, cooperation or execution.
>
> I know that when [that moment] passed, I was horrified and bewildered; I knew I had gone beyond all bounds. I had been afraid before, but now I was afraid of myself. I knew I had failed before, but this was the ultimate failure. This was despair. For that one moment of blackness, I had lost not only hope but the last shreds of my faith in God. I had stood alone in a void and I had not even thought of or recalled the one thing that had been my constant guide, my only source of consolation in all other failures, my ultimate recourse. I had lost sight of God.

The refreshing thing about Walter Ciszek is that he was never too annihilated to pray. He doesn't waste time or seek to be better before he approaches the God he has betrayed.

> I turned immediately to prayer in fear and trembling. I knew I had to seek immediately the God I had forgotten. I told him my own abilities were bankrupt and he was my only hope.

His prayer brought on an ordinary thought. I like the undramatic quality of his conversion. This was no original and penetrating insight; his faculties were not held in a moment of mystical suspension. He thought a thought which might have been lifted from the old manuals of meditation, and which in fact may have been part of his Jesuit prayer formation. He was "consoled by the thought of Our Lord and his agony in the Garden." Jesus too had experienced fear of his own weakness. Jesus too had asked "to have his ordeal removed or somehow modified."

Then in this reflection to which he had probably set himself any number of times in his religious career, a perfectly ordinary light began to burn. It was so commonplace, so unmystical and unromantic that one can almost imagine God reaching over and flicking the switch to a hundred-watt bulb in the ceiling. He was to say afterwards that this was "the grace God had been offering me all my life but which I had never really had the courage to accept in full."

He realized that each time Jesus begged to be let off, "he concluded with an act of total abandonment and submission to the Father's will." How many times had that figured in Fr. Ciszek's prayer? Yet now it was different, because now he knew from inside the character of Jesus' relationship to the Father's will. It was almost as if, being himself helpless, his will short-circuited and his faculties jammed by terror of his own weakness, Fr. Ciszek could receive into himself the experience of Christ, and could therefore understand it from inside. Inside his own being it flickered and hesitated and sprang into life, drawing his mind to know and his will to identify with it. This was a free gift of God and yet it was a deliberate act of personal choice. He would repeat this again and again, and he could never explain. Explaining never mattered. "My life was changed from that moment on."

Jesus' submission was:

> not just conformity to the will of God; it was total self-surrender, a stripping away of all human fears, of all doubts about his own abilities to withstand the passion, of every last shred of self including self-doubt.

To understand Fr. Ciszek's use of the word "purgation," it is important to read these texts carefully and see just what he was being purged *of.* We think of self-surrender as giving up our plans and preferences, being willing to accept discomfort, humiliation, contradiction. It is not common to think of self-surrender in terms of giving up self-doubt, and the authenticity of Fr. Ciszek's experience can be seen right here. After all, he had been demolished by his own acts of betrayal, had been sitting in the wreckage of his own character for four years. He had paid a heavy price for the truth about himself. You would think self-doubt was a privilege he had won, an advantage he could not afford to let go.

For what, though, was he trading it?

> I can only describe the experience as a sense of letting go, giving over totally my last effort or even any will to guide the

reins of my own life. It is all too simply said, yet that one
decision has affected every subsequent moment of my life.

It meant losing the last hidden doubt, the ultimate fear that
God will not be there to bear you up. It was something like that
awful eternity between anxiety and belief when a child first
leans back and lets go all support whatever—only to find that
the water truly holds him up and he can float motionless and
totally relaxed.

He was not sewing together his ruptured self-confidence:

I was brought to. . .this act of total trust in his love and
concern for me and his desire to sustain and protect me, by the
experience of a complete despair of my own powers and
abilities. . .I knew I could no longer trust myself and it seemed
only sensible then to trust totally in God.

He had traded self-confidence for self-doubt, but now he
realized that his terror at the possibilities sleeping so lightly in
his weakness was a want of what he had always assumed he
had—faith.

We are afraid to abandon ourselves totally into God's hands
for fear he will not catch us as we fall. It is the ultimate criterion,
the final test of all faith and all belief, and it is present in each of
us, lurking unvoiced in a closet of our mind we are afraid to
open. It is not really a question of trust in God at all, for we want
very much to trust him; it is really a question of our ultimate
belief in his existence and his providence, and it demands the
purest act of faith.

He realized that there had always been boundaries he
would not cross, "little hedges marking out what I knew in the
depths of my being was a point of no return." Yet this time he
chose to cross, "and the result was a feeling not of fear but of
liberation."

The future, hidden as it was, was hidden in his will, and therefore acceptable to me no matter what it might bring.

The past . . . was not forgotten: it remained to remind me of the weakness of human nature and the folly of putting any faith in self. But it no longer depressed me. I no longer looked to self to guide me, relied on it no longer in any way, so it could not again fail me.

IMPLICATIONS FOR JO

If Jo were to comment on Walter Ciszek's story she would probably say, "I think he's wonderful. But it doesn't work for me." To an extent she would be correct. No one's life works out exactly as anyone else's. But to a much greater extent, she would be wrong. It has to work, not only for him, but for her and for me and for everyone.

Paragraphs of *He Leadeth Me*, paragraphs which are essential to its message, can be set against counterparts in *The Story of a Soul, Prison to Praise*, Newman's reflections on a particular providence, and almost any classical spiritual work. Individual spiritualities, however varied their emphases, converge here. As Fr. Ciszek expresses it:

> . . . no reservations, no exceptions, no areas where I could set conditions or seem to hesitate. A complete gift of self, nothing held back.

Sounds awful. Let's leave it for a minute and consider a few variations on the story of Jo. It's too easy to say that Billie and Walter Ciszek had to deal with a higher degree of emotional shock than the average person. I have to look long through my acquaintance to find *any* average person. It is becoming more and more difficult to train God around the trellis of an ordered and respectable family life. We are all liable to the kind of earthquake which not only wakes us from sleep but tosses us out on the floor under pieces of broken furniture. Even the rare participant in a quiet existence has a low-key sort of wakening.

The pattern for both Billie and Fr. Ciszek was easy to see. A shock, a period of being lost, and then some kind of solution. A sleep, a waking, a seeing in the dark. For many of us, the same pattern is jumbled and unclear. We expect and demand a clean resolution. We want that hundred-watt bulb immediately and we want it to stay on.

Jo is absorbed in the demands of her family. She has a gift for being cheerful no matter what, and doesn't sit around wondering what happened to God. Every day she puts in her half-hour of quiet time for him—early, before the day collapses around her ears. She would like to think beautiful thoughts about the Bible. The spiritual facility of her friends kneads her sense of inferiority. God is a black-and-blue mark on her feelings about herself, a slow leak in her desire to be good. She knows the answer is surrender, but she can't say with Fr. Ciszek that this knowledge has changed her life. It's like a faucet she can't unstick.

What is surrender to God, she wants to know, and how do you do it? The answer is not complicated and abstruse. On the contrary, it's too simple to get hold of. Even Fr. Ciszek had a terrible time describing what he had been living by for twenty years. He tried to explain in spatial imagery, by describing first what his surrender was not.

He had been, he said, surrounded by the events and possibilities of his personal world. God was "out there," and had preferences about how Walter Ciszek was to handle that world. "Perfection consisted in learning to discover God's will in every situation and then in bending every effort to do what must be done." The events to which he addressed himself were neutral—raw material to be fashioned by him according to the orders of a God who sat and watched and was grateful to Walter Ciszek, SJ, for being such a fine executor of his apostolic projects.

It was only when this plan of action stopped working, when he realized he wasn't strong enough or smart enough to carry it out in his present situation, that his determination to do God's will in the wrong way ceased to obstruct God's desire to teach him the right way.

> I had been trying to do something with my own will and intellect that was at once too much and mostly all wrong. God's will was not hidden somewhere "out there" in the situations in which I found myself; the situations themselves *were* his will for me. What he wanted was for me to accept these situations as from his hands, to let go of the reins and place myself entirely at his disposal.

What's the difference? I want to say you can't really grasp the difference from an explanation, but only from the experience itself. Any image I can use is deficient, but you can't help thinking of a performance. The choreographer sits in the fifth row, watching as you execute his steps. You do well or you do badly and he reacts accordingly. And you don't go home afterwards for a hot bath because there is no afterwards—all of life is like this.

But the real thing is not like this at all. In the real thing, your choreographer is not out in the fifth row assessing your performance. He is your partner and every other dancer as well. He is the choreography and the energy that gives the muscles their ability to respond. And it's not a performance at all but a dance for its own sake, an adventure, a discovery, a celebration of grace. You don't want to quit because the dance is what you are and the object of your search.

What did this realization bring Fr. Ciszek? First of all, a real God. "I was being asked for an absolute faith in his existence, his providence, his concern for the minutest detail, his power of sustaining me, his love protecting me."

Hadn't he known that all along? Yes, in his head. He could have passed an exam. But his emotional drives were creating the God he could manage, whose will he could decipher and execute with a power and facility he wanted to feel good about.

What then of the self? We saw that Billie came to realize, at least to some extent, that he was valuable and lovable in himself, and through the wounds of his collapse he could enter a communion with others from which he had been excluded by his denial of human weakness. Fr. Ciszek went farther.

He realized that his bankrupt personality was the object of a concern so total that every incident, every minute detail of his life was the hushed and waiting presence of a divine desire. God was not over there giving him orders. God was within, around, beside him. It was as if the world had been created for Walter Ciszek, as if its creator could not bear an inch of space between himself and this man he so urgently cared for; could not bear that any sight or sound, scent or taste reach out to him that was not laden with his own warm and slightly quizzical smile.

But Fr. Ciszek also learned a real world. Circumstance was no longer a set of problems for which he had to find a solution. It was an inrushing personal jubilee; and he was its object. But also, and this was why he experienced not fear but happiness, it was the carrier of a strength which gathered up his annihilated faculties and set them to the task which he would have wanted to be doing all along if he had only known how. God did not repudiate the human faculties which had so failed Ciszek. He upheld, sustained, and protected him, working through the faculties from which his creature had been excluding him by a bull-headed self-determination. Fr. Ciszek could lean back on a power which would enable him to do what God really wanted of him. This was not a guarantee of constant success, but a guarantee that even want of success can be a step in the dance. His talents might be used, discarded, or partially used. His strength and ability were not the point. They did not make him, and *he* was the point.

This is what "God's will" is all about. It is not an impersonal vise, the whim of a Victorian sweat-shop operator. And "self" is not something to be stamped out or burned out until we are gutted individuals whose every thought and movement is prearranged. "Self" in the pejorative sense is simply the determination to prevent God from making us what we are, what we will be happy to be. We are not to become machines run by "God's will," but neither are we to remain machines run by the emotional dynamisms created by a love affair with what we think we must be. The will Fr. Ciszek yielded to was a will to lead him home to the joy of the person who could allow himself to be completely loved because he was completely himself.

But what of Jo, what of everyone who does not come, by a

definitive flick of the switch, to this knowledge and the ability to relax into it? For some, even many, the emotional force of the bad image of God and the bad image of self continue to generate considerable trouble. It can be very hard to want a surrender we can't feel comfortable with, to a person we don't like. Knowledge seeps in quietly, undramatically, almost unobserved. You can't put your hand on the hole it's coming in by. But then her second question arises. If your knowledge is partial, or even if it isn't, *how* do you surrender to God, and in the process, to yourself? We'll go on to that in the next section.

Before leaving this section, however, I would like to say that the experience I have called waking is difficult and volatile. It needs constructive handling. We come off best dealing with the slow and natural form in which it has come to Jo, although we do not always have a choice. Fr. Ciszek's version was harsh, but he was a very tough customer with long preparation. Life itself forced on Billie a waking that almost destroyed him. What I liked about his therapy was its natural quality. Usually we do well with a reliable spiritual director or a sensible friend.

I am not happy at all with a form of "therapy" which induces artificially and even brutally an experience of this kind. People who genuinely need professional help should be extremely careful about the kind they get.

PART THREE
THE CELEBRATION
OF
LIMITATION

WHERE WE STARTED

We reach the answer to Jo's question, by way of another. What are we surrendering to? God, yes. But God does not usually say out loud, "Here I am. Trust me." He approaches in disguise. I think that his most consistent disguise is limitation, This is where we started, isn't it? Back there with a consideration of the world which greets a new-born child.

We do not become aware of the dark in order to stay there. We wake in the dark in order to receive light. Light has a function. It shows us a day shaped by limitation, but at the same time, it shows us the meaning of this shape.

Limitation is possibly the most important characteristic of life, not because it is more important than being itself, but because what we do with it determines how much being we will be able to have. Limitation is the workshop in which we exercise the crafts of psychological maturity, but it is also the holy house where faith grows up from infancy. Here God waits, the God we do not yet know, the God who has, although we may not see it yet, torn away the stiff and ugly garments in which we have tied him up. He has thrown off what he is not and quietly waits to be noticed. This quiet is not always the ordered absence of commotion and stress; it can often be the quiet of our willingness to face and accept these very things.

Limitation is also the most obvious characteristic of life. We are people of expectation. They say that is the trouble—the trouble with marriages, jobs, retirement, the trouble with friendship and middle age. We want more than life is able to provide. There are too many hidden logs to bark one's shins against, too many curtains rotting in the sun. Everything has fences, everything runs out before we want it to. The young Anne Morrow (not yet Lindbergh) complained in a diary over her vase of dead lilac. And yet we know that a room should have flowers even though they die, and fences should be painted white. Rock walls should be planted with nasturtium or carry roses in their broken arms. A limitation is to be burrowed into. The pieces of a broken illusion are to be gathered up and cherished—not put back together like a shattered jar, but valued for their promise of something else. The breaking of a dream is the beginning of a more desirable reality.

How foolish to quarrel with the limitations of my world and myself in such a way that if neither is fully what I want I will have none of what is there. Or worse—to spend my life trying to make of both what they cannot ever be. A day of pegs not fitting into holes is a day of finding a meaning we can only enter through the loss of the meaning we are determined to impose.

Our trouble is not expectation, but disproportion between our needs and the sources from which we expect their satisfaction. That and the fact that we really do not know what to want. It is surely more interesting to get to know the world that is, the self that is, and be content to do with each what is possible than to demand of both what they cannot give. We seem to take so many years to learn that in a very important sense, we don't make life. We don't even make deals with life. We are asked to make friends with it.

Making friends with the limited quality of life—what would a prophet say to that? I know we need prophets, but I like the rational and practical prophet who forces us to stretch to the limits of possibility. I am uncomfortable with the prophet who does not recognize these limits. Our critical faculties have purposes. If they distinguish between good and bad, they must also distinguish between possible and impossible; and this will protect their freedom.

Prophets come in handy because we tend to compromise when we don't have to and choose the path we don't have to clear. A prophet stands at the crossroad and points to possibilities we haven't wanted to see. But prophets are subject to a danger we can share in absorbing their message. A prophet can be too far-sighted.

A helpful prophet has to have a good supply of reverence for the limits within which and not beyond which we can better ourselves and the world. The critical faculty can deteriorate into a condemnation of everything we do not like, and our moral indignation can become an expression of emotional imbalance. It is easier to condemn than to construct, to demand an impossible absolute at the expense of the partial and possible. We can bang our fists against a world that doesn't please us, since it is not the confirmation of our idea of what it should be.

Kinds of Limitations

Limitations come in several varieties—the kind that makes us what we should be, the kind that makes us what we shouldn't be, and the kind that just gets in the way.

The first kind forms a created being into what it is. If our eyes enjoy a tree heavy with ripe apples, we are implicitly praising limitation, for the tree has made round, red, shiny apples and decorated them with green leaves, because its nature has limited it to one kind of fruit and one way of making its own food. A child has the qualities of a child because his nature subjects him to a certain pattern of growth.

But interwoven with these natural limitations are those which nature has not given or wanted—physical, psychological and moral limitations, and the awful messes which are consequences of both. Lastly comes a category that extends from earthquakes to differences of opinion, from tragedy to nuisance. It could be described as the way things are, when the way things are is not the way we want them to be.

The first kind doesn't bother us much: we are generally content to let apples be apples. We conduct a running fight with the second group—mental illness, physical deformity, poverty, our own incapacity to achieve the fulfilment of our needs. We may have least patience of all with the last batch— the less harrowing but multiple frustrations of our control over life.

I am going to arrive at an understanding of surrender by way of the word acceptance. Acceptance is no easier to explain, but its meaning may become clearer if we describe a few of its counterfeits.

Acceptance: The Wrong Kind

Believer or unbeliever, we can become so absorbed in our emotional reaction to limitation that we see nothing else. To immerse oneself in limitation, to come to the end and remain there, making one's meaning out of meaninglessness and one's virtue out of the acceptance of defeat, can seem to be the only possible solution to life's insolubilities. By this counterfeit acceptance we accomplish a couple of very beautiful things. We refuse to unlearn our experience of awakening, and we provide the comfort of companionship for others who have come so far, who hurt so much and have so little. We do not withdraw ourselves from the company of those who know. This is the deliberately chosen, philosophically explained version of what even believers can do in spite of what they think they are thinking and more or less intend to will.

Many people find a sense of nobility in this distortion of acceptance. I think there is a much better kind of nobility. If you're going to take a chance on the truth you decide to live by, I would rather take a chance on hope. There's so much less danger if it turns out wrong.

A day is not a day because it has darkness at each end, but because it has light. A river has banks because it has water. Limitation implies that there is something there in the first place to be limited.

My river runs to thee:
Blue sea, wilt welcome me?

My river waits reply—
Oh sea, look graciously!

I'll fetch thee brooks
From spotted nooks—

Say sea,
Take me![1]

Whatever the original context of this deceptively ingenuous song, it implies a lot that people, hurt by the limitations of themselves, their world, and their pursuit of God may not agree with quickly. Even believers can prefer practical despair to the admission that there is water in the stream-bed and a sea to which it runs, a sea in which they can take some interest. There's a difference between believing in God, heaven, a universal solution, and believing in one's own personal solution. And the preliminary to acceptance may have to be the recognition of how unwilling we are to accept.

The Prayer of Possibility

The first step, what I am calling the prayer of possibility, can be prayed by the unbeliever. Breaking through the crust of a need for meaninglessness, a need for despair, it says, "My life and my world have the possibility of meaning." This can be a very great admission in the teeth of a desire to comfort oneself either by the denial of comfort, or by an unremitting anger at not having any. For some people, this admission can require

[1]Dickinson

every scrap of humility they have. They may never get beyond it, and yet they have done no little thing in giving up the absolute quality of a negation they had staked their lives on.

This prayer may seem to on-lookers the very minimum of faith, and yet for those who can see nothing beyond it, who have given up a large amount of emotional security to mean it, it is a great accomplishment. We who watch from another region of the soul must reverence and encourage it, realizing that for all we know, it may be one of the deepest acts of faith to struggle into our slick and desperate world. The negation they have thrust back in order to make it was a positive support, perhaps even the self they have a terrible need to be. And yet they are willing to let go, to say, "Meaning is possible."

Believers, who in confronting personal bewilderment, diminution, or pain, have found with Fr. Ciszek that their faith does not extend to the disaster at their own door, can also have to pray this first step of acceptance. "Something can exist beyond and even within my difficulty—something whole, good, and worth living for. However great my dependence on despair, I will not shut the door to hope."

Celebration

We can go farther, but with deliberate feet, for our object is not the quick concoction of another pious self. We can go farther by accepting the honesty of appreciation. Walking away from the desire to become our resentment, we can answer a call to acknowledge the being, goodness and beauty whose limitations have been absorbing all our attention. Let us see the beauty it would be dishonest to deny. We can spend time at it. We must. The moral and physical beauty in our personal world, in our own being, in the world at large, may be faulty and incomplete. It may flicker in bins of ash. But it is there. And we must be honest enough to acknowledge that however distorted its nobility, however inadequate its love, however disproportionate the setting of its best-cut gem, it is real.

United Nations Official Robert Muller tells the story of a personal experiment.[2] He wanted to see what the world would become if he decided to stop loving it. His experiment lasted a few minutes; he had found out what he wanted to know. The world became terrible because his eyes had determined not to see what was there. But that is not the only function of appreciation. We have been tossing about in a mystery since before we were born, and to be even a little at ease in it, we have to see with more than sight. Appreciation is more than a kind of positive thinking, certainly very different from a selective observation which eliminates the distasteful and incongruent. It is the willingness to see what is really there; but what is really there is only partially available to our equipment for figuring things out. Only God knows it as it is, and we cannot share his knowledge until he opens it to us himself. Appreciation is thus two things: the determination to use our faculties as well as we can, and the refusal to reject God's gift to them of an even deeper form of understanding. We let him tell us.

[2]Robert Muller, *Most of All They Taught Me Happiness* (Doubleday, New York, 1978).

But what have I left out? The limitation itself. Appreciation of the being within the limitation is not enough. We must also appreciate the limitation which binds and shortens and threatens to suffocate it. Limitation is a field on which the good wrestles its own negation into a rich and transcending resolution. "Terrible is this place," said Jacob. Terrible often in every sense of the English word, we are willing to admit—less willing to give over our quarrel with its geography.

But why not? Why not discover an unaccustomed happiness here, precisely here where so much no longer figures? Look what we've found—sun on the spiderweb in somebody's back alley. Even the spider isn't so bad if we look carefully at its speckled body and delicate limbs. What a bright festival is that cup of cold water. What an adventure that laugh, that bundle of old clothes, these plums, and this child's drawing.

Here we wait to be shown what we cannot figure out. This is where the question of "our ultimate belief in his existence and his providence" is most sharply put and most satisfactorily answered, even though the answers are indirect and take a while to arrive; the God with whose intentions we wrestle in the mystery of limitation, smiles as I have said, a more than slightly crooked smile. But if we can manage to smile back, we will find someone to take an interest in. Perhaps we will even find someone to like.

ACCEPTANCE OF SELF

We have seen three people discover that they were not the persons they had been laboring to sustain, that their real selves were much simpler and more satisfactory. The obvious question is how this thing I call a constructed self fits into our pattern of growth. Are our achievements just a lot of effort destined for the junk yard? And if so, should we bother?

We all know someone, and usually more than one person whose life has worked itself out into a mess, and to whom we want to minister the grace of self-respect. Professionals and non-professionals recognize that problems like drugs, sexual promiscuity, vandalism are often rooted in a poor sense of self. "Give them a sense of self-worth," we hear; and "Give them the tools for achievement, the vision that puts off instant gratification in view of something better later on." We read about workshops on goal-setting and the meaning of personal responsibility. In programs geared to achievement, children and teen-agers are being rescued from hopelessness and taught how to use the talents God gave them. All of them will make the world better for others by becoming better themselves. Are they building something false because they want the respect of other people and of their own hearts?

We know better. We cheer them. If we have the opportunity, we get involved ourselves in helping programs like this. Then how do we explain the relation between this kind of achievement and a compensatory self? The answer, as far as we can follow it, lies in the acceptance of limitation.

At first, this doesn't seem to make sense, for here are people accepting, not limitation but the tools with which they can escape a crippling form of it. But look more closely.

Constructive Limitation

First, achievement itself involves in many ways the constructive handling of limitation. We have to sacrifice the development of many possibilities in order to assume full responsiblity for a few. Because Tom Dooley chose medicine, he had to give up a career in music. Then his stern field of service forced on him an unplanned celibacy. Eventually, an early death substituted another form of achievement for the one he had chosen for himself. Responsibility narrows but deepens. We cannot develop every talent, trace every possibility. Choice is the limiting exigency of achievement.

We are limited also by our moral values. If the people we work with are determined to reach the top by means which our moral standards have to reject, we will probably not reach the top. C.S. Lewis' professorship was finally offered by Cambridge. His Oxford colleagues kept doing him in—he was too vocal a Christian. We have often to make ourselves comfortable on a by-road into which we are forced by more aggressive traffic. We have also to reckon with the common good, and with the good of other individuals. My achievement is not my private affair. It is part of other people toward whom I have a responsibility.

What we do and how far we go are also limited by a thicket of former choices, available time, and our own particular capacities. Very often our reaction to what we can't achieve prevents us from achieving what we might. We want to accomplish what we can't, look like somebody else, get a job to glitter in. Someone else is always about to clip ten seconds off the record we just set. We want the disposition we read about in books, the marriage we planned on. We would like to shed what we wish we hadn't done, and have again what we dropped on some road we can't go back to.

This is when we have to remember to look at the water instead of the banks, acknowledge all the good, the skills and graces, all the gentle and wise qualities at our disposal. If we have to search for possibilities, let us search, for limitation does not come by itself. It comes attached to being, and we are responsible for the development of that being.

The Jester

It seems unfair that something we are obliged to do can produce consequences both helpful and destructive. We saw this with the moral and spiritual disciplines. But in the case of achievement as also of the disciplines, the unfairness is illusory. It's unfair if we set up an unreal goal and feel deflated at being deprived of what we shouldn't have been aiming at in the first place. It's wonderfully fair if we realize how many answers are hidden in the wrong turns and mud-holes of our determination to foul things up.

Yes, we are obliged to achieve—or at least to try. Yes, our achievements can contribute to the balance and the healing of ourselves and our world. Yes, they can also contribute to a self we really have no business being. And the people who most need a sense of self-worth are the ones who are most likely to seek it exclusively and desperately on this level, and be most wrecked when it eludes them. Not always. For although it is easy to get caught in the cult of achievement, some patterns of accomplishment have built-in alarm clocks and periodic waking services. Their particular sets of limitation keep warning us to accept our own foolishness, to trot on and try to do better at realism.

Sometimes we muddle through with our balances slipping to one side or the other. And though few of us can survive without achievement of some kind, many of us are not so talented or so situated that we are very good at being successful anyway. What of the young woman trying to piece together a marriage she now knows was a mistake; the boy whose athletic skill has lost its importance with his graduation; the people who lived for jobs they are required to leave? All of us at some time come to realize that the sense of worth generated by achievement has helped us on one level and betrayed us on another. We have experienced its ambivalence, and the insubstantiality of the person it has made.

What are we to do then with the compensatory being who starts posing in the foreground of our most constructive projects, invades our charity and our prayer—this little guy we don't invite and can't escape? I do not want to call it a false self, this being we have fashioned from the ache of suspecting we are not. I do not want to use hard words of it, for I pity the pain that builds it, receives its confirmation from a world beyond itself, and draws breath from such achievements as can be fashioned from skills we are afraid don't matter very much. I feel sorry for this little ghost and gentle toward the need that made it.

For what is wrong with wanting to be? The nice aspect of this little joker who sits on the shoulders of even valuable achievements, is that he is an incomparable instructor in the art of becoming real. How so? How so, if he is not? Because he tells us that the worth we can construct by our accomplishments is only one level of the worth we have. If it were all, we would not have to worry about the self we want to be. We would not be constantly dreaming up and driving toward something other than we are. Achievement would be enough.

But it isn't. And we know this because the compensatory self keeps at it. With his plans, tensions; attention to effect, status, salary; his discontent, manipulation, depression at the betrayal of his interests, he keeps signalling that what we are is more accurately measured by our longings than by our skills, virtues, or intelligence. If I want to be more than I am, if my self falls short of my desire, if my world and its people cannot make for me the person I want to be, then either my desire is unreal, or something other than my skills, my friends, and my world must fit the emptiness I have become acquainted with—something as vast as what I want, something to which the world boundless is an analogy.

My longing is my one unlimited characteristic, the shape of what I really am. If everything outside has failed me, or if it has simply not done what I have asked of it, still my dogged production of an imaginary self tells me that my wants are greater than what I or others can make of myself. If there is an answer to me, it begins here. If my need is that which tells me who I am, let me listen to it, accept it, praise it. Let me see its funny, pathetic, and distorted projections not as horrors but as protestations that my limits are the voice of an unlimited destiny. This understanding of the constructed self fosters with him a peaceful sort of relationship.

We never strangle this companion; he never goes under for the last time—not until we do ourselves. Possibly he will come hopping into paradise with us, a jester and a friend. He has taught us a good deal, and rather than moan, "Oh God, not *you* again—you, strutting to the footlights; *you*, elbowing my neighbor into the shade," we might more accurately shake his hand and say thanks for digging the hole in us we know we have no way to fill by ourselves.

We can accept with more than sour resignation his transformation from foreman of our life's project to household comedian. He may still have a lot to say, but we can laugh at his antics instead of running to his orders. We are out from under once we recognize what he is doing. We can use him, as we can use every weakness in our repertory, to set the perplexity of what we are on its way to solution.

The job I'll never have; the one somebody else replaced me in; the places, people and achievements I will never have, as well as the ambitions which were more substantial as dreams than as reality; the mistakes and sins I wish I could forget; the wrinkled, commonplace present; the unreliable future—each No I take up and say Yes to is a path to a self I never thought to seek.

But how do I know?

Conversation

If our first acceptance is of possibility, and our second of limitation, the next must be of conversation—conversation with that which inhabits both possibility and limitation. We accept the gift of belief. Odd, that I should set it here, since many of us who have come this far considered ourselves believers all along. There is, however, belief and belief. This is the more substantial variety. It addresses itself to a receptivity we did not have before. The Word of God can now speak to the hole inside dug by our little friend and revealed by the brusque kindness of whatever alarm clock woke us to see it. We no longer ask questions. We are contented to be our questions, and the answers are of a different quality.

How do we know that our emptiness is the shape of eternity? Because we agree to accept God's word for it, and because the disciplines we started out with—the prayer, reading, and moral effort—have changed as we have. We are able now to listen more closely, to hear more accurately.

This is not the kind of book that tries to convince people to believe; its purpose is to tell what happens when we have. We have learned more now of what we are and aren't, and are learning more of what God is and isn't, because he can speak to a heart less defended and more real. But we must keep nurturing our faith in the same unspectacular manner— praying daily, trying to be better, to let God make us so in the quiet, practical acceptances of every day.

The disciplines we've misused may pinch uncomfortably. Because we are now aware of what we think of God, or because we may still have a distorted idea of what maturity and holiness are about, we may want to drop in shame what we have so disfigured. But what we did to them was not their fault. They brought us to the point of realizing what we were making of them, didn't they? And if they did no more than continue this service, they would be more than worth their keep.

The Grace of Inferiority

But what do we do with the inferiority feelings left over when we have done all we can to establish a sense of self-worth? This is a permanent question, for I would be surprised if the defective sense of self is something which can be wholly gotten rid of. As far as I can see, it can't be lost entirely, and a weak self-image translated into the desire for achievement, position, and affirmation can be quite a load to carry. Achievement in itself is not the whole answer to a bad sense of who I am. It can become, even when it has added one more constructive member to society, a carton of emotional dynamite.

We can be helped to handle a poor self-image; its dominance can be, if not broken, at least diminished. But in the end, we have here probably the most difficult form of acceptance. For only through acceptance can we turn this monstrous disadvantage into a road to our own reality. I believe that a poor feeling about oneself, held matter-of-factly in the transforming hands of acceptance, can create a person more real, beautiful, and helpful than the person whose emotional world is more secure and uncomplicated.

We can say, "This is part of me. I need not turn myself inside out trying to be someone I am not." We can do the possible in gratitude for advantages that time will uncover. We can spend ourselves for others as Eleanor Roosevelt did. But this is not the end of it. We must hand over to the healing urgency of God this almost unacceptable liability, and accept his way of working it into simplicity and peace.

ACCEPTANCE OF OTHERS

The far world and the near come in through different doors, and speak a slightly different language. We'll consider first the nearer one—our family, our friends, the people we work with, shop with, argue with, love and dislike—the personal world a few inches or a few miles away.

I think the limitations we find most painful in others are the ones that let us down. We have leaned, and the structure we chose to put our heart's weight on slips and breaks and buries us in broken glass—not once, but many times, in many ways. We think of the married couple who come eventually to find in each other an incompatibility so adamant that into it no communication can force a root; of friends trying to use each other as reinforcement, only to grow weary of the game each expects the other to play; of the man whose job somebody else has taken after a 20-year campaign to keep it; of the parent whose child's moral values or choice of a career come through as repudiation not only of parental values but of their very selves.

Inadequacy

The world into which we have ventured, to which we have exposed ourselves in hope and vulnerability, will not give back to us the self we need. And our experience of this disproportion between our need and the ability of others to fill it can recur as reliably as the seasons. Today's advertising encourages our expectations; most of today's literature mocks them.

The very phrase "personal relationship" is loaded with expectation, but the most detailed self-help manuals cannot make of the reality something it hasn't the power to be. We cannot be all that another person needs; and another cannot be all that we need. We have to let the people we love draw on many legitimate sources. And we have to keep trying as well not to demand of them more than they are able to give to us.

This area of acceptance requires a lot of realism or the patience to keep trying for it—or at least the acknowledgement that we haven't got it. The mechanics of marriage, friendship, parenthood, work relationships could be described almost entirely in terms of learning how to live in a world of limited people in such a way that we draw them to the full extent of their boundaries without cultivating in ourselves a discontented longing for the land beyond the fence.

Animosity

But disappointment is not the only effect of another's limitation. People can fail us with the kindliest intentions. But people can also afflict us without any kindness at all. There are such things as enemies. This is not a pleasant limitation to encounter, but it can be as helpful as any other if we know how to accept it. We all know the desperately insecure person who builds a personality out of gossip, slander, and the corrosion of other people's contentment. Many of us have been bruised by the ambition of someone on whose ladder we are just another rung. Or we may have the unfortunate kind of personality which rubs a lot of people up the back. It's no fun to maneuver in the briar patch.

A *Bigger House*

Both friendly and unfriendly limitations can hit hardest the person who most needs compensatory reassurance, for people whose experience of themselves is painful tend to demand— whether they can accept it or not—a totality of affirmation. We will want everyone to like us always, and get unhinged by the inevitable clashes, corrections, flops, and incompatibilities of a real world. To want, even to need an uninterrupted, homogeneous, and liberal flow of affirmation is unrealistic. If we study its implications, this exorbitant demand upon others ought to affect our sense of humor. That it often does not is our misfortune but not necessarily our disaster. No weakness need be that if we recognize it for what it is—a door or at least a window out of the impasse into which it seems to have got us.

For what do we learn from the inadequacy of human support but the same appreciation of our nature that we learned from our own inadequacy. The compensatory self, the clown in the center ring, turned out not really such a bad fellow when we learned to learn from him. It was only as circus master that he caused us trouble.

So, when the piers on which we parked our building buckle and slide out from under, their insufficiency only demonstrates that the house is too big for them. We need a foundation proportioned to the load it has to bear. Usually this does not mean, "I require God instead of creatures." Usually it means, "I require God, and one of the things he will teach me is the practical wisdom of how to accept the human support his providence sends into my life; how to value it for what it is instead of resenting it for what it was never meant to be. He will also teach me the way to become for others a pier that holds, a foundation that provides modest but worthy support because it is at least trying to be only what it can be, and to fit itself into the security of his own sustaining bulk."

This, my little world, is mine to accept or bear, to trust or to reject. The limitations of others can tell me, not that I am awful, not that they are, but that all of us want more than we can give each other. We know this in our heads, but coming to terms with it emotionally is very difficult. Acceptance is a slow and stumbling process, but it is the only way in which we can give and receive love instead of disillusion; healing and not bitterness; humor and not disquietude. It is not only my self which is at stake, but my ability to be of help to people who stand in need of my limited but real resources.

For if disillusionment with people we have trusted can be unsettling, the knowledge that we ourselves are failing others exactly as we have been failed is no picnic either. As we can want more of others than they can provide, so we will want to give them more than we have to give.

In the event, it is not remarkable that we have so little, but that we have so much. The great gift of life is the ability to appreciate what is there because we have ceased to demand what is not. This demand blinds us to any array of individual qualities so wondrous that, having been let in on their secrets, we will grieve to have missed out on such largesse for so long. We have not only the joy of receiving but the joy of giving joy by our receiving. We can cultivate the bare and unpromising back lot, and appreciate the harvest our appreciation has helped grow. Often it is the most limited personality which stands in greatest need of acceptance, and when we can forget what we are not getting, or how inadequately we are giving, we will get what is better on both counts—limited but real participation in the expansion of a constricted life.

The Infected Physician

I should mention at this point a particular defective way of accepting the limited personality. Prudence is a stiff and unappealing word. Ironically, it has come to signify almost exactly the opposite of what it means. In this context it indicates a clear-sighted view of what the other needs and of what I can give. Some people squander their hearts, comfort, nervous systems, and material resources giving to someone else exactly what the other does not need. Out of misguided charity and a sense of self-sacrifice, they make themselves a rug for feet which need the resistance of solid earth. They reinforce, with good intentions, exactly those tendencies which the other needs to overcome and is capable of overcoming. It's not the acceptance which is wrong in this case, but the manner of its application.

Another form of encounter with the limitations of others differs from the pain caused by friends or enemies. It approaches obliquely rather than directly. All of us sometimes, and some of us often, according to our vocation and circumstances, can fall against a variety of shin-blackeners set up by the immaturity of other people, by their moral insensitivity, the mess they seem to insist on making of their lives, or the horror that has been imposed on them by circumstances they are helpless to avoid. The suffering of others, the evil, the emotional incapacity to which we are witnesses even when not victims, can form a view of life which holds us in such bondage to the negation in another's personality that we lose the ability to heal. We are sucked into a desolation we might have lessened at least partially or whose contagion we might have contained. When the potential healer is infected, the epidemic is worse than it has to be.

We have all had the experience of provoking by accident or of happening upon or even of having to live with manifestations of profound emotional difficulty in other people, or reaction to life so embittered, calculating, self-deceived, and desperate that although we ourselves are not their immediate object, we long to shout, "Stop! Oh please, *stop.*" Some people are called by the exigencies of their career, their personal inclination, or their circumstances, to live almost totally immersed in human misery. I remember a brief contact with a group of missionary Sisters. I'm sure they were accomplishing a work of compassion, but they had caught the bitterness of the people whose oppression they were trying to alleviate. They did not realize that they themselves had become victims of the exploiting class they had come to hate; for their own hatred had robbed them of a capacity for simplicity, spontaneous and wholesome pleasure, and appreciation. Their emotional identification with the people they loved was admirable;

but the manner in which they experienced it had imprisoned them in a psychological world drained of almost everything but anger and despair. I felt that something helpfully native to their hearts had dried up and was rattling around inside. Perhaps it was inevitable, and yet Mother Teresa seems not to have hardened like this. What she offers is fresh and un-withered, supple and uncrusted. I admit that this is not an easy skill to learn, especially in a struggle for justice where the political context seems to deny any possibility of justice. It can be hard to see sometimes that the world will not be helped by our personal addition to its stock of hatred.

We can feel guilty about not being miserable enough over the misery of others. We can feel we are not truly compassion-ate if we are not reduced to desolation by the pain of our neighbor. This can be another form of the constructed self—I am more interested in being compassionate than in the objects of my compassion—but it need not be, or at least not entirely. We may care very genuinely and deeply. Because we ourselves are not the object of the other's emotional distress, because they are helpless, oppressed, or discarded by life, we may feel that any form of acceptance is a betrayal. Some forms are. But some are not. Some forms of acceptance are the only way in which our caring can exercise a power to help. And we must want to be helpful more than we want to be angry, depressed, resentful, or just nerve-wracked.

Another of the fences provided by our immediate sur-roundings can be seen in the systems to which we belong or which we observe, clash with, weep at. Systems are made by inadequate people and composed of inadequate people. I remember a sermon by one of our monks: "There's always something wrong with the monastery. There's always something wrong with the guy you stand next to in choir." There's always something wrong with something. At times we are willing to make allowances for individuals that we wouldn't dream of making for institutions. People are like eels—you can't do much with them, especially in batches. But organizations can be organized. They can be reorganized and restructured and unstructured and fixed up. They have a handle. If this doesn't work, they can be discarded, because they are visible entities which have come to stand for something with which we aren't compatible. Sometimes an act of discarding can be emotionally satisfying because we are putting into it a backlog of reactions to the imperfection of an entire hurting world—or even to a particular hurt of our own which has no connection with the faulty organization.

I don't mean that acceptance can ever be the ratification of evil—in people or in groups. It shouldn't mean satisfaction with less than can be done. It must mean a basic clarity of sight, a peace, a refusal to let our thirst for justice, morality, and goodness get cooked in the emotional stew of our own self-projection. It should issue in a practical approach to possible if not wholly satisfactory solutions and an ability to handle the human nature from which both difficulty and solution flow.

Covenant House was founded by Father Bruce Ritter as a refuge for runaway teenagers who find themselves alone on the streets of New York City. I notice how often Bruce Ritter's teens say, "You can't love me. There's something in it for you. You get a kick out of this stuff—it makes you feel like a great guy." The kid has known himself worthless and has experienced his own exploitation. He sees all of life in the light of these two experiences: I am lousy, and everyone else approaches me only for whatever can be gotten out of the deal. He isn't right, or certainly not wholly so. He can be loved for himself and helped for his own sake. But we can learn from him. Our efforts will backfire if we use the disadvantage of another to make ourselves worthwhile. There is a limit to the amount of help another person can accept from us without being turned into an instrument of exploitation in the name of charity. We can desperately want for another what is best—or what we consider best—and yet when the other does not want it, or wants even more to make independent mistakes, we have to recognize the legitimate limits which another's growth sets to our good intentions. And this, perhaps more than any other limitation, sets us in the balance between despair and the acceptance of a caring God whom we may not be able to feel and can barely believe in.

Material Objects

These too are humble presences of the principle of limitation. It's bad enough when they do no more than they were made to do, but often they do less. They sulk and snap; they break, bite, slither, wrinkle, pinch, and fall down. They can be the legitimate subjects of every verb indicating impossibility, treachery, and meanness. Occasionally, you get one that works, looks well, moves or doesn't move according to its nature. And you realize that usually, this is because you yourself have accepted that nature and agreed to let it be what it is. Occasionally we find that the shortcomings, inadequacies and malfunctions of material reality are not so unnerving after all. Material being has benefitted us in spite of and even within its resistance to our desires, because we have accepted the distress of its refusal to fulfil our need, and this acceptance has done something to us within. In ourselves instead of in the relief of a desire, we have found a source of peace.

This experience, even in as commonplace a form as the use of an instrument or acquiescence in today's weather, can give a joy and a security which are often more desirable than the possession of a desirable object. Just to know that we are not emotionally dominated by the color of the sky, the shape of a tool, or the vagaries of a machine can give us a sense—in the midst of our frustration and humiliation—of being part of a meaning which is greater than any of these things. What we usually want, in our use of material reality, is a successful performance of the self we are pushing. If we can see no farther than our need to be this self, the failure of material support inundates us with a despair proportionate, not to the importance of the situation we have bungled, but to the self we feel we are washing down the drain. Recognizing the distinction may not have much immediate emotional effect, but it rescues us from a sense of meaninglessness and eventually saves us from the most crippling of interior limitations—the need to be what we are not.

Much of Pain

I realize that the pain caused by human beings to each other can be and often is, indescribable. The prospect of an eternal destiny can be cold comfort to someone who is asking only for the strength to get from one end of the day to its other, and who can't sleep at night.

There are people whom no counsel reaches; they can only be loved. There are people who can be helped by reflection on the meaning of their suffering, because its meaninglessness is part of their pain. In successive revisions of this book, I have found myself excising the dramatization of suffering and emphasizing practical possibilities. This is not because I lack experience of pain or compassion for its victims, but because I myself have found help in this approach.

I want to be told what I can do, and I am pleased (it was not always so) to be assured that a great deal—or at least some—of what weighs so heavily on me is being generated by my own false perspectives. When pain washes over us, we can drown in it, or we can find a way to keep on breathing. I'm not talking about triumph. There are those people too, but most of us aren't they.

Most of all, we can be helped, though it may seem a stern form of compassion, to keep from adding quite as much unnecessary suffering to our burden as we generally have a mind to.

ACCEPTANCE OF THE WORLD

A distinction between the near world and the far may not be altogether accurate. Its basis cannot lie in the extent of our control over one or the other, for sometimes we can do more with the world out there than we can with the world at hand. Sending a check for famine relief can help someone a little, when nothing seems to help a workaholic husband.

Perhaps we could put it this way: In one sense, the far world is a backdrop to our struggles with the near. Like the countryside in which Thomas Hardy set his novels, it reflects and interprets the small human drama enfolded in its weather. We perceive it as distinct and yet as related. In reality, the distinction is illusory and the relation is real.

I remember a classic example of social injustice which I once read in a second-hand copy of *Natural History*. I remember it because I cannot forget it. A village of subsistence farmers somewhere in Latin America was persuaded by a rope manufacturer to convert their land to sisal. They were promised a higher standard of living; they were not told that sisal is a nightmare crop with cast-iron roots. You can't get it out.

Trapped in their tiny sisal plantations, the men must now work a full shift processing the stuff with primitive equipment, in addition to terrible hours of cultivation. Their return is low, and from it they can buy only an insufficient quantity of food whose nutritive content is much inferior to the food crops their land yielded before its conversion. The children are physically at least two years behind their age, with brains damaged from malnutrition. The man whose store sells these people cheap food at high prices uses part of the profits to send his daughters to an expensive convent school.

This is not generally happening in our personal world, although something just as bad may well be going on around the corner. It is, for the purpose of my explanation, somewhere else. As, for most of us, Covenant House is somewhere else. The world out there is a sober place, even when we are not directly involved with its difficulties. Even when our personal landscape is fairly serene, we are nervous about what might blow in from out there, saddened by what other people have to endure. We know they are our brothers and sisters and that the discontinuity which seems to exist between our lives and theirs does not exist at all.

What does it mean then, to accept the world out there? I have said that the object of our acceptance is not the evil we see, but its unseen function in the providence of God, and that we must try to keep our helping efforts from becoming one more variety of the self-assertion which is causing the evil in the first place. This means first, that we burrow into the limitation; we hold the chains with reverence, put our arms around the fence post. Not because we are in love with restriction, injustice, illness or the corruption of the innocent, but because we know there is more to the chain than the flesh it galls.

Secondly, it means that we recognize how much more there is to ourselves than righteous anger. When the Sermon on the Mount turns up as a liturgical reading, it no longer falls on the ears I was born with. Stanley Jones' analysis of Gandhi[3] has remade my hearing apparatus. I could never have drawn from these scriptural texts a campaign for the aggressive revision of unjust oppression, and yet whether or not his exegesis was precise, Gandhi was right. But he was more right in realizing that the force within this campaign had to be love and not hate; peace and not anger. I am not the one to make speeches about how terrible it is to get mad. I think most people get angry, and though many of us grow less angry or less often so, as we grow in understanding, it is unrealistic to demand of ourselves the ideal personality which never *feels* anger, either on its own account or that of others. A minister who served the area has told us of a particularly odious Times Square pimp: "My attitude may not be very Christian, but I'd like to break every bone in his body." Fr. Ritter feels the same way, and put the guy in prison. Anger is something we feel; we may never lose the feeling, and it's dangerous to pretend we haven't got it.

But anger doesn't have to determine either our personalities or our attitudes toward the limitation that provokes it. If I have a very inadequate grasp of the meaning of love, I can still put to work the little I know, and that is better than nothing. Acceptance is taking time to switch myself from a pattern of attitudes determined by hatred, violence, and anger to one which haltingly, ineptly, but with determination, opens itself

[3]E. Stanley Jones, *Gandhi. Portrayal of a Friend* (Abingdon Press, Nashville, TN, 1983).

to the creative presence of a love it cannot yet understand.

We remember Gandhi, Nehru, and thousands of ordinary people lining up to be sent to jail, and we are inclined to think of them loving oppressors who have imprisoned and afflicted them. "You have hurt me, yet I will defeat your injustice by returning not hatred but love." This is true, but we must also remember that these men and women returned love to people who had hurt not only themselves but others. It is a great thing to love the person who hurts and humiliates me; it is another and a further degree of maturity to love the person who wounds and corrupts other people.

It is I on whom acceptance goes to work, an acceptance which invades and embraces the hidden meaning in my concrete circumstance. This acceptance is not a way of saying that evil is good, that pain is inevitable, that there's no use in making myself uncomfortable over miseries which are far away and none of my business. Acceptance is a way of disposing my heart to reality, of cleaning the apparatus of my reactions so that I can love more realistically and help more effectively. For it is not the other whom my hatred breaks, but me.

I've brought love in rather abruptly, haven't I? Maybe, since the word no longer means what it is supposed to, one should never use it without a particular example at hand. We have one in Gandhi. You look at the man and you know what I mean.

You look at acceptance knowing that it involves his kind of love, and you know a little more about acceptance—but not all. We saw when considering our attitudes toward the discovery of our own and our neighbor's limitations that the temptation is to a general souring—even to what we are inclined to consider a virtuous souring. The temptation remains active on a world scale. Enjoyment can come to feel like an escape from our responsibility to bear the world's sorrow. But our responsibility to the world's sorrow should not be confused with a refusal to hope, even when we cannot understand what we are hoping for. For though acceptance involves the willingness to bear my own inability to help very much, it also demands the willingness to do what I can, *all I can*, and the effort to celebrate this privilege.

More still. Acceptance is a stumbling effort to speak the language of God, to pipe up and throw ourselves into the stream of his conversation with the world. I have said that acceptance is more than putting up with what we have no choice about. We accept because no matter how distorted the circumstance, how restrictive and appalling the limitation, we choose to walk into the mystery it hides. And still more, we proclaim by our acceptance that redemption has made of limitation—and not only the natural forms of created being but also its wounds, its ill-mended breaks, and its stunted deformations—a richer and more beautiful source of life than a perfect world would have nourished.

I am not here speaking of the good that suffering can effect in the character. Suffering has deepened many people. It has made a mess of others, but that is not the present point.

Song of the Easter Vigil

We have a need to understand things, so that however pressed our emotions, our minds at least can find relief from the frustration of not being allowed to know. Straitened by pain, they search for its meaning. The nose of the mind wants to poke out above the blankets of our distress. Explanations are available. But explanations have a way of evaporating when we most need them. Or better—their effect lies weakly on our need. This too is limitation, the photographic negative of a truth whose print is unavailable. Just as the personal need we can never fill showed us the shape of its fulfilment, so also the mental dead-ends into which our minds go running show us the shape of an explanation we can't yet understand.

They can become a comfort in their comfortlessness. For once we have laid down our demand to know, knowledge creeps in, not through the faculties we sent out in pursuit of it, but through their bafflement. Indirectly and in many unexpected ways, we glimpse the truth too large, too satisfying for the logic of our present circumstance.

We saw the need to retain daily contact with the Word of God. Revelation explains to a point. The trouble starts when we reach this point and want to dump the Revelation because it seems to have fallen out from under us, because it has left us with implications, a quest, and what can seem like warmed-over platitudes. The Word of God becomes an adjunct to our distress when we realize it cannot be domesticated.

But this is when it begins to struggle free from the limitations in which it was bound by our own preconceptions. Our trouble is panic: *we* must be wrong, *it* must be wrong. We should never have asked for meaning.

The near world and the far can magnify each other's darkness. The dreariness of a personal world may thicken the cloud cover which sulks behind it. We can color the international world with the charcoal of our own interior bewilderment. Or the outer world may drain from the nearer whatever light still hangs along its hills. Or the two worlds can merge in a simplicity of mutual distrust so uniform that we poke around in vain for signs of morning.

When most tempted to capitulate to the interpretation pressed on us by our emotional responses to so much helplessness, to so much inconsolable pain, we might read again the Western Church's great song of welcome to the transformation of its darkness. Lyrical, theological, and probably outrageous, it praises the darkness which in calling out to light, has assisted in the creation of a world more luminous and more beautiful than the one it had defaced:

> O blessed night,
> O happy fault, O necessary sin of Adam which gained for us
>   so great a Redeemer!
> Night truly blessed when heaven is wedded to earth and
>   man is reconciled with God!
>
> Rejoice, O earth in shining splendor, radiant in the
>   brightness of your king. Christ has conquered, glory
>   fills you.
> Darkness vanishes forever.[4]

This too is an interpretation. Accepting it is not a matter of yielding to a desire for emotional reassurance or for a peg on which to hang an intellect that seems to have no home. As we have seen, belief can be as uncomfortable as unbelief. The Easter Song is the kind of explanation to whose acceptance experience will lead us only when we have stopped asking, or have stopped asking with panicky desperation. This answer has a character which we consent to call mystery. It is part of

---

[4]*Exsultet*, the blessing of the Paschal Candle at the Easter Vigil; Roman liturgy.

the personality of God. And the personality of God is what is being unlocked by our acceptance. We will be told. A hackneyed phrase of something or other will flush with life, a common experience will set our eye to a crack in the fence. We will not be able to explain to ouselves or others, but the world with which we had battled, which we had struggled not to hate, has turned itself inside out and we have seen for perhaps but an instant that it is both itself and something else, that we are ourselves and something else, that the people with whom we have exchanged inadequacies are themselves and more.

Useful as are the intellects against which this world presses its unresolved imbalances, they cannot know what we most want to know until they have agreed to accept their helplessness in face of the questions most terrible to the heart. Heart will speak to heart—eventually. But no heart, least of all God's, can be heard so long as we are deafening ourselves with the clamor of our demand to know what we have determined the answer has to be. Fr. Ciszek found that out. There is a peaceful way to ask, one that counts in the possibility of being told something we do not yet know and may not even want to know. Usually we have to be very tired and very disappointed before we will shut up and wait.

It's worth it. For we really cannot use to the full our potential to help the world until we understand—a little at a time—from within, its nature and the direction from which its healing is to come. We want to yell at the world (near and far), tell it how to live and force upon it our plans for its improvement. Or when we know better than that, even the more respectful and sophisticated skills with which we try to make it better go only so far. Eventually we have either to rail at the end of our ability, or bow in the sacred precinct of the limitation.

The person who bows can say, "I will not be stifled by what I cannot do. A limitation—my own, my husband's, my city's or my world's—may seem to be a disfiguring conclusion. But it is the door to something else, something greater than the development it has obstructed. I will not yield to the assumptions of despair. I will wait for the limitation to disclose its inner nature, even if I do not see it this side of heaven. And I will continue to work."

The organizing, the picketing, the letters of protest and those of loving communication, the discipline, education, warmth, correction, counsel and dialog are all possible expressions of an inner encounter with the mystery of limitation, and of an acceptance which yet goes as peacefully as it can to the furthest boundary toward which it can feel its way.

ACCEPTANCE OF GOD

I have left God for last, since the other forms of acceptance affect our acceptance of God. It's not that clear cut, of course, because he is there from the beginning, is in on the awakening, and asks for himself the surrender we are making in every acceptance. Further, we do not check off our acceptances one after the other until we get to him: "Well, now I have accepted myself, my wife, and my world. I can start on God." But we will find in the course of trying to accept and love the daily elements of life, that our experience of God is changing.

God of the Books

The mistake would be to feel that, saddled with a phantom God, we might as well give up on the real one. We will get on with life, even with our acceptances, and put up with that thing behind the door. We are not so fortunate as the people who write the books.

But that is not true. If we begin our journey in an emotional climate which mediates an attractive God, we will have to lose our reassuring images eventually, for he is bigger than what we think we are loving. People with an oppressive sense of God seek the real one, burdened with antagonism for what he is not. People with an attractive sense of God seek him also, burdened with a desire for what he is not. And desire for the reassurance we can no longer feel is as unpleasant as resentment of the affliction we can feel.

Those whose mental attic is inhabited by a negative image of God will probably never lose it. It has taken a permanent lease. But something happens to us in the process of welcoming this unwelcome visitor. "So it's you, is it?" We grow to live on several levels at once, and this is no more evident than in moments of crisis. The God we have labored to learn from Scripture, the God we have dimly met in our life of acceptances and in our struggle to better what can be bettered, the emotional illusion of God which we would do anything to be rid of, all seem to exist at once. And a friendship is being formed, an unorthodox and unpredictable relationship in which the God of distortion becomes an element in our approach to the God of reality. God becomes the one to whom it is most natural to confide our distrust of God. The fear, the anger, and the hatred of the primeval aggressor are unaccountably pressed into the medium of a communication with the God they throw themselves against.

We probably don't pray in the words and dispositions of the books; they still get on our nerves. We don't talk about how much we desire God. But he has slipped into the position of the friend to whom we go to complain about the words we cannot use and the God to whom they are addressed. The phantom we cannot escape from has been put to the service of a relationship that eases his presence.

Something else changes—our taste. We saw this before, at the beginning of the journey when we talked about training our faculties to enjoy, to like prayer, the Bible, and spiritual disciplines. Now we meet another version of the same adjustment. Even the people with a nice view of God share this experience. They grow, if not more comfortable, at least more at peace with the loss of their beautiful sense of God than they were with the pleasure it gave them. They learn to want what is less comfortable—the bracing absence of what they used to be able to curl up beside with a good book. The people with a bad image of God have the advantage here because they never had anything to curl up beside in the first place. All of us come to prefer the quiet lines, the architecture rather than the adornment.

Ecstasy is only a stammer in the pedagogy of God. Peace is contentment in the experience of knowing more because we have accepted the insubstantiality of what is being denied us. The fast from a God of comfort becomes eventually an appreciable diet, and the negation of what we thought we needed a positive satisfaction of what we really want. This quiet God is not so bad, this unanswering voice in whose company we realize we have forgotten the question anyway.

But acceptance does more. It creates its own type of knowledge. We discover within the great and puny visitations of circumstances, a person for whom the circumstance is an instrument, a language, a garment. Coming to some kind of terms with limitation has cleared for us paths whose existence we never suspected. We have struggled to push as far as possible the kind of limit that blocks fulfilment of the world's legitimate needs, and in the wrestling match we have sometimes found our opponent is Jacob's and that he wants to be defeated. None of this meets our expectations. We do not set out to acquire a reference library on God, and often we are still so oppressed by the spectre we cannot get rid of that we hardly recognize the God we are getting. But he is an improvement. He may share the attic with his uncongenial image but we can more easily accept the God who isn't once we are engaged in a working partnership with the one who is.

God of Intimacy

Interference is not the only threatening characteristic of God. I have already spoken about an emotional resistance to forced intimacy with him. To some people, this embarrassment is more disagreeable than not getting their own way. Intimacy imposed by some unavoidable law of being can press its victim into a claustrophobic cramp where loss of freedom annihilates the possibility of relationship. Leave me *alone*. This is sometimes complicated by a false elaboration of the implications of God's nature. The imagination breaks down at the prospect of a being whose intimate love is everybody's destiny. We do not want to be the intimate of someone who is the intimate of everyone else in the world. We feel not only exposed to an intruder but deprived of the fulfilment of our very need for intimacy. We are not private any more. Earth— and worse, heaven—will give us no cool and quiet place in which to be unique to anyone.

We sit numb and resigned like a cat in a pet shop. If we don't like the God who comes in and purchases us, we can at least maintain in unrelenting feline independence the interior freedom he can never take away. He may come in, but it will be to someone who remains aloof, restrained, and ungiven.

Explanations make their appeal to the head, where the problem is not. They tell us we have no idea what we're talking about: God is so attractive that if we really knew him we would leap immediately into depth after depth of self-exposure. It would be our delight to do so. And as for being lost in a crowd, God is not the subway; he is simply unimaginable. He is all the beautiful things we have seen and wanted in this world. They could not have been beautiful if they had not been a reflection of something in him. Even whatever we desire in our longing to be unique and cherished is somehow resolved in him. He is himself the cool and quiet place we ache for.

This address to the mind may help, this caution that our emotions are being dominated by a crippled imagination, but something else may help more—the realization that God understands our reaction. He knows perfectly well that we don't know who he is, that our instincts fend him off and that though we have to be polite, we would rather maintain a few protective amenities. It's as if he said, "I know, it must be tough to be so suffocated by this thing you aren't in love with. It must be like a marriage grown stale or a friendship that somewhere has clicked off, and from which you only want to draw inward and get away." His compassion, his sense of humor, and his delicacy are not imaginary. He does not force himself on us. Little by little we find he is the kind of person with whom we can laugh about our distaste for his proximity. As with our resentment, the very thing that reacts against him can eventually become a bond of communication.

God can remove or modify this problem—or leave it with us. If it never completely goes away, what we have to remember is that just as an image of God is an image and not God himself, so our emotional impression of intimacy is an image and can distort the reality. We have picked up these feelings from human life, a very limited human life.

For some people, the experience of human intimacy is a useful and comforting road to friendship with God. But the person for whom human intimacy is an inadequate symbol for a relationship with God, especially in combination with a poor image of God himself, doesn't have to panic. This kind of person has another road into the mystery of God, and it can be the very distaste which seems to be so great a nuisance. The incapacity to accept a piece of imagery is not the incapacity to accept the reality it tries so inadequately to convey. In this case, our limitation is saying, "I know I'm not pleasant, but I'm really not letting you down. I am introducing you into the transcendence of God, taking you into that silence from which both image and concept back away in reverence. You are skipping a step in the process of learning God, and this negation of the partial is a way of entering the whole. Be at peace with the loss of comfort, for peace is greater than comfort. Your limitation is an acquaintance with infinity."

God gives us access to some images and we should accept them gratefully—I'll have more to say about this at the end. But when he denies us access to other images, he uses the denial to give us a more radical kind of knowledge. It's his business. All we know is that we don't need what he hasn't given. We don't have to be afraid or resentful or settle down into a sulk. We have traded off—or he has traded off *for* us—a lesser good for a greater, a lesser form of knowledge for a greater. If we are willing to respond to his teaching methods, we can relax and get on nicely with the way things are. And who knows what he can do to the difficulty once we stop gnawing at it, and give ourselves to prayer, to an appreciative acceptance of beauty in person and circumstance, and to generous service of our world?

God of Suffering

The doctrine of redemptive suffering, which causes so much trouble when we feel like a flock of ducks ready to be bumped off and stuffed in a sack for the sake of somebody's spiritual nourishment, can also contribute to the healing of the damage it has done. We may never surmount our basic nervousness, our sense that everything is about to go wrong because going wrong is the only good thing that could happen to us, but we can come to terms with this fear too. We're not the only ones who are afraid of pain. Fear is an encompassing emotion and we have lots of company. The fear, as a matter of fact, can be worse than any calamity that falls on us, for calamity has a way of setting up one of those second tracks on which we are able to relate dumbly and inexplicably to God. But fear is an attitude through which God has a tough time making his way.

Unless of course we accept the fear. We would like, as Fr. Ciszek did, to walk out from under it, to be freed of self-doubt as well as of the chronic dread of painful event. We fear our fear and we fear the event and we fear the kind of long bearing that we know from experience will wear out our control. God gets squeezed in between tensed muscles, and disconnected by frayed nerve ends. The person who has been hit by a great sorrow let alone a string of them, is apt to become this sort of incarnate apprehension.

What does acceptance of God mean to the sufferer who cannot be comforted by the cross of Christ, and who though he knows the theology of the Redemption, is oppressed rather than relieved by the efficacy of his own pain? Its value, he feels, only makes him a more likely target and he is afflicted by a sense of guilt at not wanting to contribute in this way to the salvation of his neighbor.

There are times when the soil of the Bible loosens up. I mean the murky and then suddenly clear trickle you get when you have been going for a long dry drink for a long dry time, and suddenly your experience finds its complement in a text you had never taken in before.

Fr. Ciszek went through this. Sometimes we do too—and often with the same text. When we have stopped or made an effort to stop resenting our own defective attitudes, the Bible starts brimming. Its brook may flow on the second level we have been talking about, concurrent with our fear. It may not wash away the fear or mitigate our resentment of the fix we're in, but at the same time we realize that Jesus too, Jesus whom we may still experience as alien and still resent, did not run gladly into suffering for others. The greatest love the world has known sprawled, shocked and bleeding, before the effort of will it took to get on with what was being asked of it.

We aren't so strange after all. Our want of what we think of as a proper religious orientation is not so great a deprivation, so immense a peculiarity. The normal people may be rarer than we think.

Jean de Brebeuf, the 17th century French Jesuit and patron saint of Canada, is one of my heroes. Victim of one of the messiest martyrdoms in history at the hands of Iroquois Indians, he could long for his capture and say of the brutality he expected that he "most willingly accepted all the torments inflicted on prisoners in this locality," while Jesus was scared to death. Jesus did not want to die on the cross; he was not so moved by disinterested love for humanity or for the Father that he could accept what was being asked of him without long wrestling in the dark. He needed time.

Fear that is acknowledged and accepted need not pre-empt forever the chair at the head of the table. We can say to it, "OK, I see you. I see in you certain advantages as well as an amount of complication and pain. I am willing to accept the distress for the sake of what I can receive from you. You give me things I could have from no other hands."

And this is true. From our experience of fear, we are learning about God's experience of being man, about man's long experience of facing a universe much bigger and more powerful than himself. With both God and our neighbor, we are entering a communion not only of understanding but of being. We are, moreover, learning about ourselves, and entering by this back door, another aspect of what it means to be true. All this is in addition to the value of our acceptance as a healing agent of the world's wounds, a value which is actual whether it comforts or disquiets us.

What we have resented is becoming, through acceptance and through the graceful action of God in that acceptance, a path to what we have been sure it was obstructing. The learning of oneself gives meaning to God's emotional unavailability, and the learning of God gives meaning to the perplexities of being oneself.

> Water is taught by thirst;
> Land, by the oceans passed;
>   Transport by throe;
> Peace, by its battles told;
> Love by memorial mould;
>   Birds by the snow.[5]

Sometimes it is even possible for people who have lost a great many of their human resources to find they are being supported by the companionship of the God who was originally their greatest burden. It happens; not always, but it can.

[5]Dickinson

PART FOUR
THE HOW-TO SECTION

MECHANICS OF ACCEPTANCE

The trouble with acceptance is that we think we know what it is and we can't do that, so we either keep trying to do it wrong or give up and go around feeling guilty.

I think the best principle for approaching the impossible is this: Cut the project into parts which are small enough to do something practical with. And when the part you have chosen to work on blows up in your face, pick up one of the pieces and do what you can with that. The principle complementary to this is one you have heard a lot about in this book: Do not lose out on what you can have because it is not what you are looking for, or expect, or know all about. Or because it doesn't feel the way it should.

We all know what acceptance should feel like. Then we can't sleep and we know we are not abandoned, and our irritation at not being abandoned keeps us awake when the original tension might have been done in by the body's insistence on rest. What we wanted actually was not acceptance but the feeling of having accepted, or perhaps the feeling of owning a psychological gimmick for transcending the pain of our problems. What we are being asked for instead is acceptance of the difficulty of acceptance, or at least of not being able to make it feel the way we want it to.

Acceptance is something we can always do, but not something we can always feel. There's a difference between an action and a state of emotion. Am I being asked for a definite particular thing which I know I am refusing? Or am I just lost in a fog of feeling that I am not accepting, not abandoned, not much good? There's so much we don't like about so many things, so much that can intensify the fog. Why not break it down? Let's make friends with one aspect of our world which we wish were different—something very concrete. Not, for instance, a difficult person, but one small trait of that person. Then we can assign ourselves a few definite moments during the day to let down our hands and stop fighting it. Too easily we can let ourselves slide down the drain of a big, general sense of not being able to accept the whole mess. Of course we can't. But we can accept one thing, or make a consistent effort at it; and that one thing will affect other things. At any rate, it is certainly better than the gurgle at the bottom of the drain. Acceptance is God's work in us, we are laying ourselves open to his surprises. Who knows how good at it we might eventually become? But we won't have a chance if we feel we have to tackle the whole thing all at once.

What we're accepting is limitation, so we have to accept the limitation of our acceptance; even the limitation of maybe never feeling that we're good at it. This doesn't mean we are then free to snarl at everything but the matter of our project. It means that we are trying to free our acceptance from an emotional dependence on doing everything right. The further our acquiescence can expand, the happier we will be, but if we demand of ourselves a global resignation, we won't have a chance to begin. God has reasonable expectations. We should cultivate them also.

Having said this, I have to add that for myself I have found that the more I accept with praise—ragged as the attempts may be—the better off I am. Even if it means an encounter with how little I want to accept. To say, "This is not an affliction but a present. I will learn its name eventually and know what it really means," or "This is my small personal opportunity to live in the spirit of non-violence, to increase the stock of love in the world by absorbing a modest attack on my sense of self," is to unify my efforts. It grounds them in a single attitude.

I know I would be even better off if I were quicker to get at it. All sorts of constructive sermons to myself don't do for me what the cast of mind behind praise does. When I start a slow and quiet concentration of the mentality of praise, when I get *at* it, something goes to work which wasn't there before. I know the difference. I'm no longer trying to do things on my own.

Earlier in this book, we considered prayer and the spiritual disciplines as forms of acceptance. They are also roads to acceptance. To the small account I have given of these in another book, I want to add here a kind of supplement for the desperate.

Prayer

One of our problems with prayer is that we are asking too much of it. We have perhaps read or heard somewhere that prayer will mend a defective personality. Daily immersion in prayerful transcendence of our emotional tensions will heal them far more effectively than fooling around with examinations of conscience and campaigns for moral improvement.

There is some truth in this and some falsity. The truth is that we need prayer for healing. There is no substitute. Fr. Ritter tells his associates that his demand for prayer is non-negotiable. Mother Teresa's Sisters say they could not sustain the emotional load of all the misery they deal with if they did not have their daily hour of silent prayer. Often after a history of failed effort to improve dispositions, attitudes, or relationships, the mud will dry underfoot and the fog clear for miles—because we have kept praying. The effects of prayer as well as of the perspectives it reveals are healing effects. But when we examine the periods in which we most grew up, what do we see? We prayed, but we did something else too. The grace came—how? Not as a result of our moral effort as the tractor runs when the mechanism is correctly operated, but as a result of God's operation in our action, our prayer, our failure, our acceptance and our willingness to go back and try again.

We all know people to whom we would like to say, "Forget your conscience. Think about God. Think about others. Forget your stupid faults and wriggle out of the shell that has been hardening around you since the day you were born." We also know people whose devotion to prayer has been absorbed into a faulty personality orientation and if we dared, we would say, "Stop *praying.*" We would be wrong, but understandable. Then there are the people who expect prayer, and sometimes a specific type of prayer, to mend the cracks and fissures of their characters, and who retain without realizing it, ravines of such depth that, if we had any hope of being heard, we would plead, "Look, *this* is wrong, and it's hurting other people. It's hurting *you* and impeding the good you could do for the world. Please *do* something. You *can.*" (OK. Maybe you can't, but you could at least agree to *see* the thing. You could let God use it to deepen his relationship with you by inhabiting your good natured tries and flops.)

The human personality is wonderfully complex, and no one of its activities can absorb the functions of the rest. Prayer cannot supply for other responsibilities. The most effective attitudes toward life are the ones which give us a simple way of dealing with our multiplicity. We can easily remember to get into our lives prayer, study, and some practical moral effort. We give these elements their unity by looking at them from a single vantage point. This keeps us from splintering off in a frenzy of trying to keep track of our component parts.

I have chosen to express this unifying element as surrender or acceptance. The very same attitude is also called praise. For St. Therese, the unifying attitude was love, but we are not all capable of putting as much psychological weight on this base as she could. For the kind of person this book is discussing, love for God can be more an implicit reality than an explicit objective. The theological virtue of charity is not always recognizable to beleaguered emotions. Our misapprehensions of the place of prayer also imply the need for competent guidance when this can be obtained—even if only to tell us now and then that we're getting on everybody's nerves.

People who have to pray to a God they don't like may be less concerned with what the prayer should provide than with how to put in half an hour of anything at all. They just want to stay awake and concentrated—on *what*, is not important, so long as it passes muster as reasonably germane to the project. Someone like this has often gotten beyond the stage of enlisting prayer in a drive for the reinforcement of a constructed self, and just wants it to be worth something—anything at all.

Within a three-part prayer method of vestibule, inner room, and door to the world, here are a few suggestions for people whose prayer is complicated by emotional resistances to its object, and who sincerely want to walk the road of acceptance:

Quiet Prayer

This form of prayer by its nature can give us a taste for something better and deeper than our usual psychic traffic snarl. It can give us a taste for a God we can associate with silence and tranquility. By using a neutral prayer word which suggests quiet and does not arouse negative reactions to God, we can find in this kind of mental peace (if we can get to it) another face of God, one we had never had a chance to dislike.

However, the danger lies in a kind of "transcendence" which prevents us from working through our emotional jungle into a real clearing. It can help to solve the problem of God, but it can also deceive us into thinking we have, when we have not. We should use it; but we should also keep our wits about us.

Stairs

This is not nearly so complicated as it might sound on first reading. It is not an exercise of the imagination. Imagination goes to work on the background; the background then becomes so familiar that we do not need to think of it. It has become the shape of the prayer.

This is a technique for people who are really in a pickle, though it may work for others also. It changes the vestibule or preparatory section of our prayer period into a stairway. We situate ourselves mentally on the first floor of a house, where we are being knocked around and yelled at by our tensions, angers, activities and habitual emotional attitudes. Our room for prayer is quietly waiting for us upstairs, but here we are, the captives of a whole lot of stuff we wish we could get away from. This is simply a way of concretizing the state many of us are in when we set ourselves to prayer. Wanting to be free is its chief characteristic. Or is it?

Here we have one of the discoveries of this form of prayer. Are we held captive by the negative forces within, or do *we* hang on to *them*? If we could get rid of them, would we? There is a stairway leading to the prayer room above. We could climb it if we liked. It has (You determine the number—I use 21 but five or ten might work better for others.) stairs which we climb one at a time by laying on each a single element of the throng by which we are afflicted. We lay it there by accepting it.

What could be wrong with us? What do we need to give away?

Guilt: I smashed up someone's day by my bad temper. I manipulated a situation in such a way that I emerged the innocent victim of someone else's bad temper. I blamed someone else for my incompetence. I have a chronic and far-reaching personality clash with someone I have to live with; or I don't want to pray at all because of some more spectacular moral problem I can't get a handle on.

Worry: My friend, my child is in serious difficulty. I know how to fix it, and *I* have to do it, and I have to do it now. No matter that I'm helpless in actuality. I do the repair job over and over in my imagination. Or unemployment, debt, sickness—any or all—have become my total emotional climate.

Discontent: I hate my job, my house, any one of the thousand limitations we have been talking about.

Humiliation: I've made a fool of myself and have to replay the scene in a starring role, saying the lines I only thought of an hour later.

Inferiority: A daydream may be relieving the chronic pain of being me.

A sorrow, a serious failure, an ambition running wild—one by one, I can choose to lay each separate element of my emotional disturbance on a stair, leave it, wait a bit in quietness, and go on to the next. Or perhaps the surrender of one element takes more than one stair. We don't have to cover every element of every disturbing factor in our lives—or even of one. Perhaps a small part of one problem can become the prayer of today's climb:

This irritating habit of so-and-so.
This inability to do well what I so want to do.
This person who is going to get my job.

The climb can be leisurely. Quietness can in fact overtake us early on. Then we just stay there, absorbed in the mystery of our problem's unknown inner being. We may be able to rest in it and reach beyond it; or find contentment in accepting the humiliation of being so bothered by it.

Or the climb can be swift. We would like to reach the room, and just walking deliberately up and out of the mess can be enough. The important thing is to realize this process is a prayer in itself. It is not a way of making ourselves good enough to pray.

There is a room at the top. The symbol of an inner room appeals to me because what we are walking away from and shutting out is not something outside ourselves but something inside. There are inner doors that have to be opened and shut. How reluctantly we often climb the stairs, how hard it is to relinquish worry and anger and planning as if our world would disintegrate if we let go for half an hour.

But something more than that is wrong. This mental jungle is the construction of a self. It may be agonizing, wearying, stifling, but the weight, the worry, the anger and the calculation are making *me*, and I can't bear to let them go. I'd be so much better off without all of it, but then I would have no one to be.

The stairs will never be a perfect job of letting go, but they can get us into the habit. When we get to the room—if we get to it—we will have dumped a lot of garbage on the way up. Never mind if it comes oozing in under the door. A human being is trying to pray. We are desperately anxious to save the only self we know about, and we need a long time to be content with the self we are. God understands better than we do.

A fireplace in the room may center us on a fairly agreeable symbol of God. Or a breeze at the window in summer. Once we have opened the door, entered, and deliberately shut it, we can here use any of the prayer forms recommended for the central portion of the prayer—quiet prayer, rosary, *lectio*. Perhaps something on the stairs asks to be continued as the prayer of emotional honesty. Perhaps we have found it helpful to write out the stairs very slowly, or briefly in code words, and now even in the room, we find a pen helpful. Whatever helps.

This method is not a way of locking ourselves into ourselves. It is the opposite—a way of turning even massive emotional barriers into a form of communication with God. We should be terribly honest. God knows it all anyway. He knows, for instance, that we often don't want to offer him our anger. The last thing in the world we may want is for him to go to work on it, perhaps to take it away. If we have been afflicted, our anger can be our only consolation. We want to make things as bad for him as they are for us. Whether he or someone else is the object of our rancor or jealousy, the emotions can cause both pain and the easing of pain. They burn and they satisfy. The anger may be more desirable than cessation of the pain which feeds it. We don't want to yield the emotional satisfaction in exchange for the lesser good of losing the pain.

This method has another function, and facilitates another form of acceptance. We can use it to celebrate a particular joy, a personal object of thanksgiving. Or we can use it in the contemplative rumination of some aspect of the mystery of our salvation. It can be tied in with the liturgical cycle. In this aspect it is a slow savoring, a progression to the silence of a mystery which we are to reverence in the simplicity of the upper room. But it must be just as honest. It is not a way of preparing ourselves to put on a good show. It is designed to lead us out of self-preoccupation, but this should not be by way of trowelling over the chinks in our emotional plaster as though they did not exist or should not show.

As for the last part of the prayer, the return to daily life, I have to leave that to you, according to where you are going from the prayer time. Usually, I just get up and go, but that seems deficient.

Stations of the Cross

The Way of the Cross can be made in silent prayer or in a kind of *lectio* which leads to silent prayer. Its flexibility, its built-in focus on the Passion, even the physical participation it invites, are particular advantages.

You may like some of the books on the Stations. There are many. Caryll Houselander[1] and Hubert Van Zeller OSB[2] have done less conventional treatments. There is also one by Hans Urs Von Balthasar[3]—kind of heavy, nice drawings. You may be better off making your own book, or using one which is, theoretically, unrelated. I have made the Way of the Cross using at each Station a few lines of one of Merlin Carothers' books, Eliot's *Four Quartets*, or Paul's letters.

[1]Caryll Houselander, *The Way of the Cross* (Sheed and Ward, NY, 1955).

[2]Hubert Van Zeller OSB, *Approach to Calvary* (Sheed and Ward, NY, 1961).

[3]Hans Urs Von Balthasar; drawings by Joseph Hegenbarth, *The Way of the Cross,* (Herder and Herder, NY, 1969).

Our grounds keeper John constructed a Way of the Cross in the woods. You really walk it—up and down and around. It is full of meaning in late winter when the buds have begun to swell, but the passage of seasons is an important part of it at any time. One day, when it was occupied by someone else upon whose prayer I didn't want to intrude, the idea came to me that I didn't need a ready-made set. Why not start just anywhere and use any likely tree or rock formation that turned up? (I got lost at least twice.) Several times I wound up at our very symbolic brook for the last Stations. (Some people add a fifteenth Station for the Resurrection; others feel that this is richly implied in the entombment.) Sometimes fallen trees come in handy for the three falls, and groups of trees for the group scenes. Nature gets a chance to put on a Passion Play. But you don't have to finish if it's obvious that God is somehow meeting you at one particular turn of the road and you are inclined to linger.[4]

If this kind of thing appeals to someone who doesn't have a woods and would feel silly making the Stations in a park, there may be substitutes, providing you have an understanding family or can hide out from them for a few minutes. Windows, pieces of furniture may do. Some people make a little booklet for commuter trains and buses—the pocket Way of the Cross.

---

[4] I am obviously approaching the Stations as a framework for prayer, and as such any old tree will do. If Catholics are concerned about the charitable application of an Indulgence, they might be able to work something out with little blessed crosses. Columba Marmion OSB had a set. He made the Stations every day of his life with the exception of Easter Sundays.

Lectio

I wish I could conduct a survey among people who resent, dislike, are indifferent to, or even hate God. I would like to know whether the negative reaction persists, or persists in undiluted strength, during the time of praying with a small section of the Gospels. In other words, does the presence and personality of Jesus mediated through the Gospels evoke the same resentment as the psychological spook in our emotional attics?

Some people have had unfortunate experiences with the Bible, so that Scripture itself is a problem for them. They may also associate it with poor religious art. But Scripture has real curative power, and even if we have to keep working at a technique of *lectio* in order to open ourselves to it, we must do just this. There is no substitute. Be at ease with the text, or be at anger with it—whatever is natural. Ask it terrible questions, fight with it, laugh with it. Often, evidences of Jesus' own sense of humor splinter the solemn language. I have a friend who likes a paraphrase (*The Way*[5]), some people learn Greek, and *The Good News Bible*[6] is a lively translation with nifty drawings. As we have seen, our own experience delivers up the meaning of deadly-familiar passages when we have cradled them in the quiet of our anguish or our joy.

[5] *The Way* (Tyndale House, Wheaton IL, 1971); Catholic edition (*Our Sunday Visitor*, Huntington IN, 1973).

[6] *The Good News Bible* (American Bible Society, NY, 1976). There are two editions—one with and one without the deuterocanonical and apocryphal books.

Other books can help too. Try the fine biblical explanation of The Redemption by Wilfrid Harrington OP, *The Prodigal Father*[7], and his *The Bible's Ways of Prayer*.[8]

Things to Look At

I mean pictures—photos, paintings. I also mean architecture, sculpture and the natural beauty of growing things, birds, and rocks. What we look at may have no overt religious significance—and sometimes it is more effective when it doesn't—but this does not make it profane. Only we can make it profane by denying its nature as a celebration of the divine exuberance. We have to learn how to look. Some people might be helped in this educational project by a book on haiku. We have to practice letting what we see still our agitation and bring us peace.

I have used for meditation at various times a guide book to the White House, illustrated books on American Impressionism, Eastern icons, architectural history, Belgian villages. We are all familiar—too familiar—with the current fashion for photographic meditation books. I don't use them, but the principle is not bad at all. If wonderful books are too expensive, borrow them from the library for a while.

The one guideline I would provide is familiar: we should stick with one object of attention and frame it in a quantity of time. If we dash from sight to sight, successive stimulation will increase instead of diminish our agitation. Attention to sun

[7]Michael Glazier Inc. (Wilmington, DE, 1982).

[8]Michael Glazier Inc. (Wilmington, DE, 1980).

and shadow on the planes of a building can wash our faculties in visual simplicity. We can learn to select and frame details in our visual field as a photographer does, eliminating clutter and entering the quietude of single objects or simple relationships of line and form. This exercise can intercept currents of worry, anger, and fear; it is easy to learn and fits any spare few minutes. We don't even have to rummage in our pockets to find it.

Projects

Some people have ear attention. I leave them to their own initiatives. Others have eye attention and I am one. But I also have something else which someone may share—hand attention. Other cultures encourage this. I think that some of us at least are impoverished by a world of abstraction on the one hand and ill-made everything on the other.

If it helps to use your hands as well as your eyes and ears, use them. Projects can be a supremely satisfying way of chewing through barriers. Collect and copy (and illustrate if you like) texts you would like to keep on your night table or pray from at *lectio* time. Ask Scripture a specific question. (What are the ways in which various people approached Jesus? What does it mean to be poor?) Hunt out answers, making a workbook of it. Can you carve or mold? Sew, draw, knit, or embroider? Make collages? Do carpentry? How can your (even modest) skills be developed in this kind of project? God will come to meet you in the enjoyment of your creative potential; there are projects for cooks and projects for people who go nuts over the annual migrations of birds. You can integrate trips to the art or science museum or trips to the zoo.

How about the very obvious project of getting to know God through acquaintance with as much of his beautiful creation as you can encounter in the course of a particular period of time? On some days, this can be planned and recorded and celebrated—beauties of nature and beauties mediated through the creative achievements of the human imagination, mind, and hand. We do not automatically see what is there. We do not automatically love it. This was the conclusion to Robert Muller's experiment. When he decided to stop loving nature,

> The beautiful Hudson River became an unnecessary, ugly mass of wasteful water, eternally and boringly renewed for no intelligible purpose. The trees turned into senseless grotesque parasols fighting in the air with the leaves for a little solar energy and with the ground for some moisture and chemical nutrients. The flowers seemed vain, the crows were killers, the squirrels were vicious ... my joy was childish, my job was senseless, my entire life a wastebasket filled with despair, hopelessness, and death at the end.
>
> Emerging from this ... experiment and shaking off its last ugly images, I found myself once more confirmed in my old, intuitive belief—that only one recipe can solve man's problems—the law of voluntary, determined, conscious love for life and for the world.[9]

Here we have the word love indicating a deliberate decision to accept the beauty of the world.

I should go back here and pick up the people with ear attention. If you don't know much about music, why not find out more? (Even if you have eye attention). Think of what

[9]Muller.

you're missing. Think of what God is missing from all the appreciation you don't give to all the beauty you could love and don't.

People

We can collect people in various legitimate ways. Try notebooks in which people you know are listed with every virtue, talent, enjoyable quirk of personality—your own kind of small biography. Dig for every grain of good and pile it carefully. Then list the shortcomings which most bother you—*with* your understanding of how they came to be and how these handicaps magnify the worth of the accomplishments which they have made more difficult; and maybe how they are helping *you* to grow.

This kind of book can be used for prayer, a prayer in which we enter the sacred place of another's human deficiency and wait quietly as God helps us to identify with the need and the beauty of another person. We can almost become the other, feel the shackles of someone else's weakness on our own hands, experience the magnitude of someone else's small triumphs as our own.

We can get to know well-known people living or dead, by reading and taking notes on a series of biographical works or material they have written themselves. This kind of acquaintance can get rid of a lot of our own mental cramps. It is well to enter an understanding relationship with the limitations of these people as well. There really are a few ideal people in the world. They are usually off in corners. But people with unusual gifts and big personalities have shortcomings, and when they are public figures, the shortcomings are public too. This keeps us aware that our life's concern is with the graceful handling of imperfection and not a play for flawlessness.

Collections like this can open to us unexpected areas of ourselves. We will become aware sooner or later of the perspectives from which we habitually view other people. If we keep seeing the same defects in others, the problem may be less with them than with ourselves. Certain personality traits in them are pressing against vulnerable areas in our own emotional tissue. Our own efforts to compensate for inferiority, to ram the world into a machine we can drive, are threatened or frustrated. It's interesting how many faults in others we can accept, laugh at, or even enjoy if they don't scratch our own wounds. Certain relationships can make it impossible to relax with someone: "She'd be an enjoyable, colorful character if she weren't my mother."

Since lists like this convey an impression of agitation by their very abundance of possibility, I have to caution again: Don't so overload and disperse yourself that you damage your own capacity for receiving and enjoying. Learn to go slowly, to absorb deliberately, to choose among the possibilities and to discard with abandon. What we eliminate is as important as what we take on. Go read some of Anne Lindbergh.

Study

This applies as well to study. We have to beware of the "There is so much to learn" syndrome. First we need a simple grasp of the framework, with the most important pieces in their proper places, then we can fill in, continuing at a contemplative pace, cultivating a talent for depth and simplification, rather than desiccating ourselves in a wind storm of facts and ideas. The amount of knowledge we really absorb is the amount we are able to put to work in our life experience, and this will vary with the person. We want the kind of knowledge that becomes flesh and fiber of our relationships, our patience, our gentleness, and our reverence for the mystery of life; not facts dried, sorted, and tinned for exhibition.

We have to remember also that study is not prayer, though it can become so, that projects are not prayer though they may open the door to it. If the door opens, walk in; don't be so driven by a need to finish that you forget what you wanted in the first place. All this stuff can be fun; it's meant to be an experience of the fun and beauty of the real God. But we shouldn't be so derailed by its interest that we substitute it for the regular period of prayer.

Other Disciplines

Having treated these at cheerful length in the *Laughter of God*, I want here only to caution the person subject to despair, depression, and resentment of God to make liberal use of the most joyful forms of ascetic practice. Asceticism should make us better company for other people, ourselves and God. This does not mean, as you have been hearing rather often, a face-lift to eliminate perfectly normal inner wrinkles, but the cultivation of attributes which too easily get trampled on in the determination to be an impressive religious person.

ACCEPTANCE
AND
MAKING THINGS BETTER

How do we reconcile responsibility with acceptance, how keep one's heart free of a spirit of criticism while working to change what is deserving of criticism?

Most of us have at least a few friends who seem to give a lot of their spare time to helping someone else. We also know people with just enough time and hardly enough money to cover their personal and family responsibilities. Their field of service is the job they hold, their family life, the people they meet in the supermarket, garage, or neighborhood. The daily run of their lives is what they have to offer to the reconstruction of a world that has fallen on bad times. We also read of one person after another who has decided something can be done with a particular situation and has done it—some on a broad scale, some on a very modest one.

My point is that our acceptance can take many forms but it must take flesh. We can look at all we can't do and come down with a case of despair. Or we can do what we can without bitterness, and with the willingness to laugh not only at contradiction, but at ourselves.

In answer to the original question of how to reconcile acceptance with the labor of healing and rebuilding, I want to say, as usual, that we will understand only by doing—or that we will not understand until we have poured our acceptance into a particular need. Unlike water in a bowl, however, acceptance gives shape to the activity it inhabits. Perhaps we already have all the activity we can manage. The task then is to infuse the work of building or healing with the warm resilient humor of an accepting heart.

Or perhaps we are being called to take on further forms of service which our labor of acceptance will make clearer. In either case, the experience of letting acceptance grow into ministry will help us understand why we must minister with acceptance. I can indicate a few reasons, but reading the words is an inadequate substitute for the experience itself.

First, the limitations we are seeking to erase, broaden, or rearrange have a purpose in our own development. The limitations I want to assault with anger have something to give me if I stop to converse with them. No matter how warped and evil they may be, they address themselves to the limitations of my own heart. Limitations tend to play themselves off against each other. Am I so sure the zeal with which I am attacking what I see as evil is wholly disinterested? Are there not elements in my reaction which may be identical to the evil in the forces I combat? My style, my arrogance, my self-righteousness, my assurance that everyone else's judgement is inferior to mine—do I like these qualities in me? What if the evil I am fighting goes down to defeat out there only to triumph in my own character?

But what if, even to begin, we have to push our way through a forest of cultural and psychological differences? Acceptance makes us receptive to how much we are learning instead of angry at the need to carry so much frustration. What a beautiful thing is the friendship which can sustain the hurt of temperamental and cultural difference in a love deeper than the confirmation of one's own identity.

Considerations like these can help to soothe the irritations, even the agony of encounters with corruption, impotence, or confirmed self-destruction. But they are not really answers. Fr. Ritter's salvage rate is 30%. No answer will comfort the people who lose the rest. They are laboring at the mouth of a sewer in a dark and suffocating mystery. They supply for answers with little words like, "Not even a sparrow . . . "

It is not enough to stand beside the evil, the ignorance, the depression or the anger and manipulate their component parts until the situation works right. We must work from inside, and we get inside by acceptance. What we accept is the mystery and the meaning within the mystery. How we accept is gauged by our ability to do the work, not for the nurture and furtherance of our compensatory self, but for the good of those for whom we have undertaken it. Our acceptance is not a personal way to become ourselves through the vindication of our way of looking at things. The other's need is not a stage for our heroism.

We reach into the need, the injustice, the mental or physical poverty and embrace its hidden meaning, the mystery beyond sight in which its horror is resolved. And we accept our inability to understand. In this stretch of the heart, we find ourselves within and not beside the difficulty we want to heal—within and not beside the cross whose value as an explanation we may not even like, and within this very dislike which is our way of embracing its meaning.

Guidelines

The guidelines for our active ministry to the needs of others are obvious ones. Their application is less obvious, because everything we undertake gets sucked into the complications of our restricted ability to handle life, and because the problems of the world are themselves so complicated.

We are going to be facing our choices from a variety of perspectives. The girl in high school wondering what to do with her life has a wider range of choice than a married man whose previous choice has trained him for the career in which he has begun to advance. A couple entering their retirement years enter new opportunities for service.

Growth, as we have seen, is a process of attaining depth through narrowing of choice. The choice of this work or that, marriage or single life, these friends, this life-style is going to determine the pattern of responsibility within which a social conscience can express its concern for the world. It's a pity, in one way, that we must make so many radical choices so young. From the standpoint of ten or fifteen years' experience, we may feel that this is the wrong job, the wrong husband, the wrong home and the wrong mortgage. Sometimes we are able to change a life-style without jeopardizing the family's future; usually we have to continue to choose from within a framework established by past choices, and this is not a pity at all. The acceptance of where we are is our response to the sacrament of limitation.

Balance

Every guideline starts here, with what we call today the recognition or establishment of priorities. First things first. If we have chosen marriage, we must keep room in our lives— and ourselves—for the person we married and the children to whom we have given life. Our work is also a responsibility of this primary sort. It is a trust which we should be handling with moral and charitable sensitivity. Our way of earning a living, our family life and the manner in which we use material goods give us a daily array of opportunities to enrich or impoverish the world. Our prayer life comes in on this level. Without it we are diminished and deprived. We will be less and give less, and never be able to accept anything at all. This is all so obvious. And it usually is being said by somebody who can't understand why it doesn't seem to work for us.

Time

For how many people is time a friend? To the sick, the old, the discarded and the dispossessed, time can be the incarnation of their sense of uselessness. It's strange, they feel, that anything so empty could weigh so much. To the rest of us, time is often the most active of our daily limitations. It can be the principal reason why our priorities get lost in the scramble, the parent of the scramble itself. Biographies could be written of this one intractable opponent of our good intentions; for usually it is within a running argument with time that we have to work out our vocation to service and explore the possibilities of love.

Possibilities

We feel that if we could beat time to its knees, could get a little more organization into our day, we could make a dent on what needs to be done for our neighbor. On the other hand, we know that all the time in the world won't make a dent on what needs doing.

This is where the familiar principle of possibility re-enters; it is never far away. In fact if we have any sense at all, we never lose sight of it. In this case it reads: Do not be so discouraged by the magnitude of the disorder that you fail to take advantage of small, possible ways of lending a hand. If there's something practical you can do about time, do it. If you can't, listen to what the limitation of time has to say to you, and do the possible.

What can be done? I can't tell you. All of us must take a look at the view from our own bend in the road. Some people have opportunities in the very broad field of what could be called political activity. Some can make good use of a movement or organization which by pooling efforts, can make the most of everyone's scraps of time. Much social reform is built into ordinary life: How do we buy, eat, invest, dispose of waste, treat the rest of the environment, drive, worship?

An interesting economy can attend our efforts. Two or three good intentions can walk along together. Families can have projects that build family and world at the same time. (I know—this kind of thing sounds good on paper, and invites a book by someone who has tried.) Many projects have multiple goals by their very nature. I have read of a woman who founded an organization to combine anti-abortion work with work for nuclear disarmament. She has a triple end in view, for she hopes in this way to resolve a polarity of attitude which sets these two movements in alien camps.

What about friendship? Law, necessary as it is, can never recognize human dignity as it deserves. Can't our friendships cross racial, cultural, and social barriers? I know someone who started a "book club." Each month its members read an agreed-upon book to discuss at their meeting. If groups like these are more than "people like me," and their members more anxious to learn and love than to display superior opinions, they become places of growth on several levels at once.

Even the most pressed and harried life has room for little things. In fact we might not be so harried if we had a way of helping others that gave us at the same time a sense of creative pleasure. Some people are good at drawing out the talents of others and coordinating their work in such a way that the person is not subordinated to the quota. This is one of the most valuable skills given to human life, and we should all keep practising at it.

There remains the service given by those called to sacrifice active service—or at least its more obvious and satisfying forms. These are the people whose ministry to the world seems hardly to emerge from its center of prayerful acceptance, because they are mentally or physically ill, radically disabled, or even helpless from poverty. Or they can be people, like contemplative Religious, whose life-style by its nature is a silent ministry.

This inability to "help the world" in a recognizable way can be a form of service. These people should first make their own private list of opportunities. They will probably find a gold mine of possibilities. Even the seriously sick often have a surprising number of tasks proportioned to their strength—

the smile with which they receive the help of others, an interior surrender to the need for help. Cheer—the attractive kind, not the tense and artificial kind—or the effort to be cheerful and serene, can make the localized person a pleasant place in which others can come to dunk a bad day. Disabled persons can achieve an amazing degree of independence, and give to us out of inner resources greater than our own.

We have to realize that there is no way in which we can be deprived of some exteriorization of our inner acceptance. The dying person is a sacrament of the ultimate meaning of life. The comatose child or the victim of Alzheimer's witness to the mystery of a life within. Some people are deprived of activity on one level so that on another they may say to us what only this deprivation can say: that what we are is the importance of our life, and what we are is a small piece of creation in which eternity is at home.

Time does not figure much in this kind of mathematics. In our mourning of untimely deaths, we have to remember this. Desire is the measure of who we are and what we accomplish. And desire itself is often a hidden and mysterious guest whose face can only be uncovered in eternity.

The reader at the end of this how-to section could easily feel that the how of acceptance is as obscure as it was when we started. I have said, "It is not this," and the hows have been walking on side streets instead of the main avenue. The reason for this is that acceptance is based on an attitude, a way of knowing, of trusting the good concealed in what appears only uncomfortable, unjust, or essentially tragic. And anything we can contribute to this underlying attitude contributes to acceptance.

Acceptance is not something for which I or anyone can give precise directions, because it is that moment of the heart in which faith, hope, and charity disclose their patient visitation. Everything we do, though necessary, is oblique to the gift. All our practicality, enthusiasm, and humor is accomplished in the power given by these formidable walkers of the main road. Saying yes, stammering it or maybe forcing it out of clenched teeth is part of the process; but the yes which emerges from seeing life as deserving of acceptance is evidence of the ultimate gift. In the end, we will see just what it is that our yes has been accepting, when our eyes are fully opened and our yes is absorbed into the gift.

PART FIVE
ENDS
AND
BEGINNINGS

SUCCESS

Wanting can be a terrific nuisance. The mechanics of wanting can confuse our efforts at acceptance or our efforts at anything else. C.S. Lewis describes this confusion in a passage on erotic love:

> Everyone knows that it is useless to try to separate lovers by proving to them that their marriage will be an unhappy one. This is not only because they will disbelieve you. They usually will, no doubt. But even if they believed, they would not be dissuaded. For it is the very mark of Eros that when he is in us we had rather share unhappiness with the Beloved than be happy on any other terms.[1]

Some people have this precise kind of trouble because they are constantly attracted to somebody. But almost everyone has trouble with the horizonless quality that any desire can take on. Desire for inconsequential objects can cause a disproportionate amount of the pain of life. We may be impaled on a want—an undistinguished mediocrity of a desire—which is

---

[1]C.S. Lewis, *The Four Loves* (Harcourt, Brace, Jovanovich, NY, 1960).

not really a longing for the object but for the emotional effect the object promises to have. The object is to some extent unreal, and to some extent infinite. We experience it as the answer to our need. It is not the job, the success, the material thing, even the person we want. It is to be. This thing we want, this relationship or salary or reassurance has value because it will make us feel valuable. And the commotion over getting it is proportionate to the real object—one's self, one's being, one's life. We struggle for it as we would struggle for breath under water; we feel that this loss or this imposition is the affliction that nothing could ever repair. If *this* could be mended, then our world would put itself back together again.

Strange how often this happens, and in the intensity of our distress we forget last week or last year. We forget the many things or people whose loss turned to benefit, and the events which with equal intensity we *didn't* want and had to bear and now are grateful for. The mechanics of this emotional nuisance are too clear to miss, yet we do. We have wanted like this before and we will again. Yet in the wanting stage, this thing at hand is the only thing we could ever desire and its loss a devastation.

Occasionally it can be. A profound change or the loss of a deeply loved person initiates a process of true grief, and we have to stick with the process until we come out on the other side. But for the insecure, grief is too frequent an experience. These squalls that hit with hurricane force—it would be well to say, "Let's wait a day or two." Let's play for some distance and see how things look on Tuesday; help somebody, have a collection of to-do-in-a-crisis activities that will cut the emotional current. We could exercise physically, make something, keep a book around that helps us laugh at ourselves. Most of all, we could expect to compound the difficulty by making our usual mess out of bearing things bravely; and know that the shame of this will increase the desire.

Our own incompletion has in the end to be accepted. No matter how well we manage—and often our success is more apparent to others than to ourselves—we will feel the emotion, and struggle to escape the interior clangor. "They like to drag you into an endless argument," Ransom says to Lewis, who has sustained a barrage of assaults against his determination to do something he does not want to do.[2] It is better not to let oneself be drawn in. Take note of how the process works and don't think you can win the argument. With true grief or superficial grief, thoughts are emotions in disguise—in fact, the one driving emotion of wanting ourselves to be.

Success

The desire for success can be as ravaging as any human want. I have spoken of success as a good, but also as a building block in the construction of an unreal personality. It can be either. There's nothing wrong with success. Each physical step we take is a type of success. The baby becomes a member of society in a series of successes. Most of us would do badly if we had to spend a lifetime being bounced against the wall of failure. The danger lies in what success can mean to us and the extent to which it determines our emotional weather.

Some people have to take the risk of serious failure in order to accomplish a great and necessary work. They have to

[2]C.S. Lewis, *Perelandra* (MacMillan, NY, 1945).

compete on a grand scale, and sustaining loss as well as gain can be good for them. It is not always mature to avoid competition. On the other hand, we can have such an emotional involvement with the great risk that we can't survive if it lands us in the trash can. We ought to have in addition other interests, other goals, modest investments in which success is easier and failure less of a devastation. We must learn the skills and enjoy the rewards of teamwork, of contributing a share to the common task. Surely we must live in fidelity to an inner life; without it we cannot establish and maintain enough proportion to keep success from becoming our narcotic. But inner life is usually not enough. God expects us to use our common sense, to cultivate balancing factors in our lives.

Often the progressive awakenings of the spiritual journey show us how adroitly we have rearranged our desires and exchanged the pursuit of one form of success for another. We may have curtailed the size of our house, we may even have given up the prospect of career and marriage and embraced some form of the Religious Life. Then we realize we have substituted for success in the corporate world, success in the spiritual world. We cannot bear to fail at being mature or spiritual or self-controlled.

Few people set out to provide us with role models in failure. It's just as well; this might not be too healthy an ambition. But we could use a few. I have often wished I could say this when the failure of a spectacular attempt has piled the pieces of a human being by the side of the road. "Look, your present service to the world is greater than the kind you wanted."

I'm glad the emotional smokescreen which obscured Jimmy Carter's policies, personality, motives, and character has begun to thin. His administration is being reevaluated and he draws

well when he speaks. But that is inadequate compensation for
the particular pain with which he has had to come to terms.
He felt God had called him to the presidency as to a kind of
ministry. He wanted to implement a number of highly moral
values. Instead his work collapsed on his head. At the 1984
convention he was an embarrassment to his party, because in
our culture failure is a greater disgrace than moral degenera-
tion. You don't give prime time to someone who threatens to
drag you with him over the edge.

"In my most private moments, I ask God that my life not be
wasted." When the Carters left Washington, I wanted to say
to him what I have often wanted to say since: You were right.
God called you. He took you very seriously, seriously enough
to give you a vocation more important than the one you
thought you had. He didn't interfere with the factors which
blocked your efforts. Instead he touched your failure and your
pain and made it a source of healing to people who desperately
need you to help rebuild lives broken by expensive failures.

Our world encourages, advertises, demands, and rewards
success; and the constructive acceptance of failure is not
recognized for what it is—success of a more radical kind. The
values Jimmy Carter wished to express through the presidency were good ones. But he shared with the rest of us a value
which was to bring him a lot of pain. He wanted to do good,
without realizing how badly he wanted to succeed at it. He
floundered emotionally, fought bitterly to retain the presidency, had in the end to accept defeat, humiliation, and an
extraordinary amount of personal abuse. His was no emotional summer squall, but the deepest of agonies, and the
dignity with which he has borne the destruction of his hope is
a greater achievement than a successful presidency would

have been. It is something more rare, more profoundly moral, and more helpful to us.

I would want him to know this, and not to care too much about things like his library and conference center. I'm glad he continues to serve, to speak for his ideals; we need to hear what he has to say. Acceptance of failure does not mean giving up, but continuing to contribute from whatever position we seem called to occupy. But our contributions must be held lightly lest they become compensations for losses they can never really replace. His greatest service is not, helpful as it is, what he has to say about peace or the environment or human rights, but his share in the redemptive failure of Christ. We need to see that the relationship with Christ not only supports a man in his bearing of unhealable hurts, but eventually proves itself more desirable than the original object of his desire, and more sustaining than the vigor of an unwounded heart. God did not persecute him; God gathered up the pieces of what would have happened anyway and put them back together more richly than they were before. We need to see this.

He has something else to give us—the witness of his beautiful marriage. I am impressed with the depth at which he and his wife have participated in each other's suffering. The book she wrote has been praised for its large-mindedness, its charity, and its reflection of her beauty of character. Perhaps her pain was even greater than his. She speaks now of the journey they had to make, and made together. This marriage, enriched by its share in the cross, is, in a world of burnt-out relationships, a quiet place to rest.

To know that God's activity is not hampered by our failure, that the disruption of our most admirable ambition is not a betrayal of his interests is to begin to understand the nature of success. We need a certain amount of it. As we grow, we will learn to need less, and we will see that the difficulty it can cause us is based on the way we are using it to satisfy emotional needs. As a drug, it has all the harmful effects of any drug. If we can accept it with pleasure, lose it with bruised humor, come to some kind of terms with the pain its loss inflicts, it may become an asset. If my personality has loaded me with an inordinate need for success, I have to recognize this as a disability in whose mystery I am destined to learn. Learn what? I will not know until I have faced the problem as a problem in myself and not in the world which seems to deny me what I want; until I have faced, accepted, and tried to make of it the kind of road to the kind of reality we have been talking about in the course of this book.

Sports don't interest me much, but its people can. Occasionally my interest is caught by someone whose character is revealed by a career in sports. I have admired tennis champion Chris Evert-Lloyd for her goodness and equable temper, her willingness to keep at a competition which she no longer dominates. It is not easy for her; she is frank about that. She may retire soon, but to her also I have wanted to say, "Your vocation is not tennis. The meaning of your life is not this physical and mental skill you have perfected. It is the poise and generosity with which you can lose, can step down from first place, and not go off in a pout." Her grace in this difficult adjustment is a far greater gift to us than her past achievements. After all, how many people in the world can be first at anything? We need someone with whom to identify in the process of learning that being better than somebody else at something or other is not what makes our life important. To excel at competition does not make me who I am.

Knowing this and living it is a moral and spiritual achieve-ment more valuable than success at any skill. In our daily encounters with hurt and discouragement, somebody's tennis record is not going to mean anything. It might even mean precisely the wrong thing—that the value of life is coming out first. But the generosity with which an individual like Chris can handle and put to the service of her inner growth this experience of diminishment will comfort our struggles to break free of a disordered need for success—while our vicar-ious share in her technical mastery might encourage rather than heal our desires for an unreal self.

I saw in a clipping the famous photo of Mary Decker Slaney's angry and anguished reaction to the loss of her Olympic gold and I wished I could give her something else to want. I wished I could reach inside and turn off the terrible desire that owned and tortured her. A little piece of metal had become an identity for this child of a broken home. This is our world, isn't it? Not Mary only but so many of us lie on the grass raging at what we cannot have. She was more obvious, that is all. And is what we want any less ephemeral than the ability to run 8/10ths of a second faster than somebody else? God looks across at us with grave eyes and says, "Child, you hurt yourself so much. You are afraid of *me*, but it is not I who hurt you."

It would be dishonest to imply that Mary and others so burdened can surmount this emotional difficulty simply by recognizing it and applying a little will power. Life is not like that. We can come to see that getting what we want doesn't stop the wanting. The want is a hurt that never gets better. We can moderate, redirect, understand; we can walk into the teeth of our storm. And still we grow discouraged when the healing seems slow and partial.

A personality has been shaped around the goals of success or pre-eminence; the personality does not quickly or easily unlearn itself. And now our trouble will be a desire for the success of freeing ourselves from an addiction to success. In this as in many kinds of trying, we will have to accept being limited to the slow and steady, the set-back and the going-on, the conversation and the carrying of bruises and burning wants to a God who understands perfectly well how much we want to be wonderful; and that we are, although not in quite the way which currently appeals to us.

IMAGE

Who am I? We said in the beginning that we could be told and yet had to spend our lives finding out. An answer can be addressed to the mind. But what you already know can still be waiting for you along the road of a personal hike on which you and your world are soaked in the sweat of your acceptance, your prayer, and a growing relationship with the companion whose proximity you may not always have appreciated.

Truth is not a personal fabrication. But the absorption of truth into this one life is your adventure. I cannot do it for you; nobody can. The job is not arbitrary, but it is unique. The truth which watches beside you in a moment of critical need, which uncovers another level of meaning in an experience of joy, or slowly forms an attitude toward the disruptions of a personality you are trying to create—this truth differs to the touch from the theological propositions your mind has learned to control. Study is a pleasure and a duty, but study is ancillary to being. It is the backbone which keeps us from collapsing into a lump of subjectivity, but bones are not a body.

We can learn about the Redemption, but we only begin to understand it when we recognize the refined quality of our betrayal of a friend; or our eagerness to trade someone else's need for a round of personal applause. We have to experience what we are not in order to appreciate what we are. But limitation is nobody's name. Only in the light of what we are can we understand the meaning of what we are not, and see that our limitation is being transformed by what it limits.

And what is this? It is more than the compassion we learn from accepting our own weaknesses, more than our ability to give our flawed being in friendship. We can be told about this more. We have been told in many ways. Here, I want to consider only one of these ways of knowing ourselves, and see something of how it looks after the head has accepted it and the whole person has gone off on an expedition into its mysterious simplicity.

"Let us make man in our image and likeness," says the God of *Genesis*. In one of the many texts which tradition has given to its enjoyment of this notion of our dignity as images of God, St. Bernard adds:

> Why should the soul not venture with confidence into the presence of him by whose image it sees itself honored, and in whose likeness it knows itself made glorious? Why should it fear his majesty when its very origin gives it ground for confidence?[3]

Right here it must be admitted that I have chosen to use the doctrine of the Image because I like it, even though it raises a

[3]Bernard of Clairvaux, *Sermons on the Song of Songs*, Vol. No. 53 (Cistercian Publications, Kalamazoo, MI, 1979)

few difficulties. First, the original statement is not conceptual but imaginative. (We have faces of which an image can be made and so we speak as if the eternal Father had one too.) And if you try to be precise, you find your tongue knotted around "the image of the Image," which is miserable language. Second, the theological elaborations of this theme are multiple and complex. Third, it is almost impossible to avoid using the further imagery of a mirror, an imagery which is variously used, as you will see when it crops up with an entirely different sense in the next chapter of this book.

I am going to deal with these annoyances thusly: Get around the first by being imprecise, the second by letting you know I am oversimplifying, and the third by admitting that I couldn't think of a way out of it. We will use mirror in one way here and mirror in another way later, and the difference will be obvious.

So we are images of God—each one a portrait, a mirror, all of us disreputable little puddles in which the accidents of daily existence ripple across the face of eternity, pools spreading from the mouth of a divine spring. Here in this water which wells up quietly from a source beyond any place, I can read the riddle of my life. Bending to see my face in it, I find the face of God looking back.

That is the simplest way of saying it. But there is more, and some of this is said by Paul when he speaks of Christ as "the image of the invisible God, the first-born of all creation." He is the mirror in which we gaze to see our features in the face of God, the spring in whose waters mingle eternity and time, God and creation, need and abundance, limitation and the absolute.

But why should this sitting by a pond turn out so grand a

climax to so serious a hike? If after all I don't have any interest in God, I can hardly be blamed for resenting a destiny and an identity which seems to have dragged me around to my starting point. I don't want to be an image of God. I want him to go away and leave me some pleasure to forget him with. And I don't want to be important because I am Christ, but lovable and interesting because I am me.

It Has a Name

Yes. But if we have walked the road this far, we know our complaints are not what they were in the beginning. They are by now almost conditioned reflexes, growls and snaps without direction. We don't intend to bite, but we haven't yet developed a satisfying substitute for the bark. The knowledge our intellect has accumulated may or may not have increased much, but our way of looking at the things we always knew has been severely modified. Our laughter at ourselves may be rueful but we know it's appropriate. We know we're no worse off than anybody else; we are in fact much better situated than a lot of people we know.

Our discontent, the emotional cramp in our relationship with God has a name, a name we have learned to accept along with the blistered nerves and sore feet we got along the way. The name may not be congenial but we can see the joke in our own distaste for it: the name of our antagonism toward God is the cross. We dislike the word, and sometimes the reality it signifies. Our dislike is based on factors already discussed and on a history of encounters with books and preachers who portrayed the Passion badly, interpreted its position in our lives without sensitivity to our emotional difficulties, and forced it on us when we had developed no inner capacity to understand or receive it correctly.

Now we have to face it as the bridge between the two great facts of our being—the emptiness and squalor of what we are not, and the limitless marvel of what we are. But I said more than that, didn't I? I said that our antagonism toward God, our weariness at the bearing of guilt and the futility of substantial improvement, our discontent with the general short-sheeting of life are themselves the cross, or at least forms of our participation in it.

Consider the person who has come to pray or who is in the process of picking up the rubble left by the latest collapse of a serious effort at self-renewal. Is it easy to confront the God before whom we want to appear poised, well-dressed, and well-behaved? Is there no barrier to crawl over, no limiting obstruction? Maybe not, for some people. But for some, the barrier is obstructive enough and immovable enough to require more than the development of a technique for prayer. Distractions are not always the lure of an attraction we prefer to the presence of God. They can be evidences of an unwillingness to accept as helpful the limitations of our nature and of particular manifestations of it: I feel that what I have done wrong should not be; what I want and cannot have should not entice me; the phantom of a God I cannot like should not obscure the God I have to face; and what I do not want and am stuck with should not tie my nerves into knots.

The trouble does not lie with all this, all that should not be wrong and is, but with my failure to acknowledge that even its obstructiveness has a function in the development of what St. Bernard calls our glorious birthright. Our weakness, our stupidity, the compounded stupidity of a world which seems to set limits to everything but its capacity for smashing up its own future, all the negations we have been cataloging in these reflections—these have a name and it is the cross. Our acceptances have value not because they pacify our emotions but because they set us within the power of the cross.

We have our own ideas of nobility. The naked Christ, we feel, was clothed in something better than the ravelled fabric of mismanaged opportunity that is our life. He might have been emptied, poor, and helpless, but he never lost his greatest possession—his moral stature. No man is poor who is, as he was, rich in moral excellence. What kind of entry can we make into the sublimity of his offering? How can we even relax with someone so unrelentingly good?

It is not our history of negation or our present weakness or our inevitable future failings that clear the mirror of our likeness to God. It is this history, present, and future *accepted*, and by that acceptance raised on the cross and then buried with Christ. For when, by acceptance, we allow them their Easter, they become the hopeful, homely virtues of simplicity, love, and humility. Yes, we're sorry. Of course we are. But when our sorrow takes on the practical consequences of acceptance, consequences such as those I have been outlining in this book, we can slither under the constraining barriers we were not able to climb over, and go dashing around like a bunch of colts whose pasture has suddenly lost its fences.

The moral beauty of Christ is not an obstacle if we agree to relinquish the feeling of inferiority we develop in the presence of any sublime character. OK, we feel puny, soiled, and unlikable. But our virtues are going to be built precisely on acceptance of our need for strength, goodness, and beauty. To accept our negations is to accept our need. The dazzling moral beauty of Christ is not a spectacle by which to be dwarfed and humiliated, but a home in which everything belongs to us. We should not resent the beauty which so emphasizes our deformity, for we can knock on its door and walk in and appropriate it all for ourselves. Our claim on it is that we need it, and our key is the acceptance of our need.

Virtue is not just being good. We can, as we have seen, be good in a totally unsatisfactory way. It is being true. And to be true we have to be humble, to accept that perhaps our outstanding virtue will always have to be the picking up of pieces and the making of new beginnings. But also to accept the fact that small, cheerful, and persistent virtues have a value without limits, for they are gifts of the cross of Christ. The smallest of puddles still holds a rising sun.

The cross is not a dreary prospect standing between us and the enjoyment of life. It gives to life its enjoyment. It absorbs our failures and frustrations, our evil and our regret for our evil. It welcomes the acceptance with which we have to return again and again to its arms with less than we want to bring. It will always cherish the continuity of our effort, our broken bones and noses out of joint; for, held in acceptance, these inconveniences are not what they seem to be. They have become truth, hope, faith—and whether we are willing to admit it or not, whether we can recognize it or not—they have become love.

There is no question of choosing between a pleasant life and a life with the cross. We're going to get life whether we want it or not, and our choice will be whether to bring it to the cross or let it go on banging its head against the one thing that could have healed its bruises and drawn out its truth.

All this has an interesting implication. If this is what we are, we can start from here. Not chronologically. Psychologically, most of us must work our way toward it. But when we can grasp, at least partially, the unlimited value each one of us has as an image of God and the function our very dislike of God can have in sweeping clear the mirror within, we can keep coming back and back to this genuine source of our own worth. Here is the center from which to encounter our world and to accept our emotional sense of inadequacy. It has always struck me as unfair that self-confident people find it easier to be humble. The secure personality has less fear of losing the kind of support an insecure person needs so much. The people most sure of themselves can often be the most self-forgetful. Often but not always.

Self-Forgetfulness

I remember a day in the woods when I lay for awhile on the ground looking up. This was on the recommendation of Ivan T. Sanderson in the book *The Continent We Live On.*[4] He says it is the best way to look at a tree, and I really like beeches. Very naturally drawn out of myself by something as bright, fresh, and even uncommon—seen from that angle—as sun in the beech leaves, I hated to get up and put myself on again. At this stage of our spiritual journey, we can find that the search has led to a way of knowing ourselves which gives us a genuine

[4]Ivan T. Sanderson, *The Continent We Live On* (Random House, NY, 1961).

chance to forget ourselves. No matter how ragged and unreliable our feelings about God, the world, and ourselves can still remain, we have learned our own basic truth. We have seen through the answers we thought we knew and perhaps have wanted—but didn't dare—to reject. By letting the Word of God inhabit our experience of life in various practical ways, we have found a security compatible with the squeaks and stalls of our unfortunate psychic machinery.

From a dignity we try to dare to believe in, we can lessen our grasp on the things and people we have pressed into the service of a makeshift sense of worth, seeing them less as adjuncts to our project of self-establishment, and more as sharers in the image we know ourselves to be. It is not a magical transformation. The person whose wizened personality demands unique and primary status will come to accept a smaller role in the lives of other people, will realize that being even one small part of a group that supports someone else is a privilege, is to be needed and helpful. The wobbly personality may still desire center stage, but it can take the pain of this unfulfilled desire and lay it simply on the dark threshold of a morning it can't yet see approaching.

The pain may still remain. We may have to begin over again the next hour, the next day; it may require a great effort to keep trying to be happy on a shelf with a collection, but we know that in ourselves we are unique and cherished, beautiful and gracious. We can afford to give, to accept, to live contentedly within a world of limits and to be a limited self when we know that those limits are the cross on which our personal journey spans the distance between a self we cannot bear to be and a self that matches a limitless desire.

Do we still feel no emotional attraction for God, for the face which looks out from the mirror as our being and our destiny? The God in whom our beauty has its source? It either doesn't matter, or it matters much less. Attractiveness is a medium. When we possess—and know we possess—the reality, the medium loses interest because it is so much less than what it stumbles in trying to convey.

I think that forgetfulness of self is more than the result of a prayer technique, and that the journey to it involves, for most of us, more than an unself-reflective type of prayer. We can begin to crawl out from behind whatever barriers are protecting the self when we know this self to be valuable not from what sticks to it from outside but from what it is inside; when we know that even our weakness and betrayals need not violate our beauty—can indeed be transformed into a humble perseverance which increases it. Self-transcendence is a nice expression. What we think it is and what it really is do not always coincide. I think that, like happiness, it is a by-product, something which slips in unnoticed when we have forgotten to want it. We see it in its psychological form and feel attracted, when this may be for us the most effective obstacle to having it in reality. Most probably it can only be reached (whether or not we feel we have reached it) by way of accepting what looks like a series of roadblocks to ever getting there.

As for discontent with being loved for the sake of Christ and not for ourselves, that is the kind of distress that eventually goes away because we have stopped trying to talk ourselves out of it. Like so much else, it can't be talked away. Someday it will just not be there any more.

Prayer of the Image

To have spoken of the support this doctrine can provide for someone who has always had a problem with God is not realistic without the search I have been describing, or at its beginning. It would be like trying to plant a geranium in concrete. Anyone who has had the experience will know what I mean. Truth can be intellectually accessible and psychologically impossible. Even now, at this stage, there are for individuals, differing degrees of accessibility. I would like to suggest another type of prayer which may be helpful along the road.

It fits into the same three-part framework and is a variation of quiet prayer: I simply look down into the stream that bubbles up from God at the roots of my being, and see the unseeable features of a face I know to be mine as well. I remain still in that moment of recognition, no longer needing to keep up the fight to be somebody. I accept the gift of my own worth; I agree to be beautiful.

This can also be done with the rather more seeable features of Christ, whether in a material representation—an icon or the face of the Shroud—or in a general and quiet memory.

It even has a handy variation which we could call the prayer of the photographic negative. With a title like this, it hardly needs an explanation. This is the prayer for the moments when we feel ourselves least like, or most unlike the God whose image we know ourselves to be: I am the negative. Quietly I accept myself as that, knowing at the same time that the negative contains the image—*is* the image in a state of waiting to appear. Very simply, we expose ourselves to the light.

None of us is alone the image. The celebration of our own worth is the celebration of the world, of all we stumble over and fail to see by, of the outgoing tides and the minds that cannot speak to one another, of every element of the creation which also bears the features of Christ.

I'm sure heaven will be pleasant. But there is one great pleasure we will have to leave behind when we are there. And this is the relief we can find in knowing that it is no longer important to be important. After a journey like this, or in the course of it, the knowledge that we can safely be one insignificant dot on the canvas of a pointillist painting and still relax in a personal significance that no one need know but ourselves, is one of the greatest joys available to the human spirit. There must be some eternal tongue that speaks this language.

AFTERWORD

> Exultation is the going
> Of an inland soul to sea—
> Past the houses, past the headlands,
> Into deep eternity.[5]

Heaven. So much suffering has no other resolution, and no one's life has meaning except in relation to heaven. But eternity is unimaginable, and the imagination never starves quietly. It invents terrible heavens, nightmares of bright space in which all the people who ever lived stand forever with their elbows in each other's ribs. Or it pictures fulfillment as immobility. This effort to imagine the unimaginable erases shadows, weather, three-cornered conversations, morning, evening, noon, creative work, and all the other good gifts of limitation.

Heaven has been a classic subject for meditation, and this is right: confidence in the future can make our handling of the present more gracious, our acceptance more constructive. Yet

[5]Dickinson. The poem is split between the beginning and the end of the chapter.

something in us resists, something more radical than not knowing how to do it. We distrust it as a betrayal of our responsibility to the world we see. We love the earth. For all its disadvantages, it has the character of place, and we need place. The earth is our project, our challenge. And it is beautiful. We dislike the kind of other-worldliness which distrusts the legitimate pleasures of earth as if each beauty tossed away were some kind of credit toward a heavenly reward. Some saints would seem to have welcomed death because they had made their earthly condition so exceedingly uncomfortable, and because heaven was the only pleasure they could want without feeling guilty.

We can't junk our repugnances to this form of meditation just because we know they don't make sense. But we would do well to recognize them for what they are—a species of emotional prejudice—and we would do better to stand up to them. Realizing this world is not the last stop for the 70% that slips away from Covenant House will lessen our despair but not our practical concern. Knowing we will, before too long, become everything we've always wanted to be and more will help keep us from turning other people into blobs of wax in which to press the stamp of our individuality.

It's true that our view of heaven can be deficient but our view of most things is deficient. A faulty attitude toward pleasure is a faulty attitude. It's going to be there whether we think about heaven or not. An attempt to think correctly about heaven is a way of facing up to the faulty attitudes which the thought of heaven reveals.

But how?

There is, first of all, quiet prayer, in which we are not bedeviled by the imagination one way or the other. But, for one thing, this does not last all day, and for another, the imagination is not a low-class faculty. It's an instrument of evocation, poetry, and myth; not a lesser way of knowing but often a fuller one. Fuller than abstract thought, which we also need, fuller sometimes than the state of its own transcendence. If we learn to ride it, we won't find ourselves so often squashed beneath its hooves. For some of us, this can ask a certain humility, the relinquishment of a feeling that we are less successfully spiritual to the extent of our imaginative involvement.

Our knowledge of the transcendent has two tributaries: one says, "Heaven is not like this", and one says, "Heaven is a little like this only make it as vast as you can." We don't have to confine ourselves to either. God became man—for one thing—in order to reach us by way of limitation. We don't have to be afraid of taking him up on his offer. But neither do we have to get stuck in the kind of imaginative representations that stifle rather than free us for communication. We can find ways of acknowledging ourselves as imaginative beings without being so tied to the image that we cannot rest in the stillness the image can evoke.

Since I am ending a book, not beginning one, and since this particular theme would need a treatment of its own, I can only indicate a few paths for exploration.

One Easter morning, in the numb and beaten state of having gotten through Holy Week, I went into church before Lauds. The Paschal Candle was quietly burning, symbolic object of the Vigil celebration. Almost, I thought, it has been waiting for me.

We are accustomed, or some of us are, to attend upon the Passion of Christ, offering presence to his dereliction. We are less interested in attending upon his experience of Easter. I mean here *his* experience of Easter, not merely an enjoyment of creation because creation and we ourselves have been transposed into an Easter key.

Of course we can't imagine his experience, not in the sense in which a novelist can construct the emotional state of the characters. But we can make ourselves conscious of one or a few of the great evocative elements in the Easter story:

Morning

Have we ever really studied the coming of the light—sat or walked outside in that greying hour between night and day? *Spring.* Do we live in a sealed concrete box? Avery Dulles' conversion was vastly affected by the buds of one small tree swelling into leaf beside the Charles River in Boston. Or the *Paschal Candle.* It's there for almost two months. The Easter Vigil does not exhaust the possibilities of its service. Learn how to pray by looking.

If we enjoy particular pleasures—music, the dance, the weather, a time of day, people, fireplaces, dogs, cats, or horses—we probably would be more helped by letting the sense of pleasure and completion these bits of creation evoke carry us into an appreciative quiet, than by torturing our imaginations into tossing everything we like out of what then becomes an overheated, overcrowded, overlighted vacuity which feels less like heaven than hell.

Whatever gives us joy in these humble companions of our

earthly journey is a weak reflection of the God we will enjoy forever. Enjoy. Not endure or tolerate or suffer from. And though there is more to heaven than wild geese and symphonies, I suspect that only in heaven will we properly appreciate the pleasures we are here tempted to consider insignificant. We think of our friends who have gone ahead, "They have God now. *This* can't make them happy anymore, this trifle, this view from a bend in the road whose ending they have reached." Don't be too sure. Perhaps only now can they savor it fully. Perhaps they are happier now sharing our small happinesses than we are ourselves. The end of it all can't be less glorious than the best of what we have loved along the way.

When the Narnian children reach heaven in *The Last Battle,* they mourn for the country they have lost, for "all that lies dead and frozen behind that door." Then they find that "Narnia is not dead. This is Narnia." Lewis compares their experience to the earthly one of seeing a landscape as it is and then in a mirror:

> As you turned away from the window you suddenly caught sight of that sea or that valley all over again in the looking glass. And the sea in the mirror, or the valley in the mirror, were in one sense just the same as the real ones: yet at the same time they were somehow different—deeper, more wonderful, more like places in a story: in a story you have never heard but very much want to know. The difference between the old Narnia and the new Narnia was like that. The new one was a deeper country: every rock and flower and blade of grass looked as if it meant more.[6]

[6]C.S. Lewis, The Last Battle (MacMillan, NY, 1956).

Then as Lord Digory began to mutter about Plato, the unicorn cried out what must be one of the most appealing statements about heaven ever made to people who love the earth they were born to:

> I have come home at last! This is my real country! I belong here. This is the land I have been looking for all my life, though I never knew it till now. The reason why we loved the old Narnia is that it sometimes looked a little like this.

There is consolation too in the gift of Pan to the two animals who had enjoyed his melody and his presence in Kenneth Grahame's *The Wind in the Willows*. As he vanished into the rising sun, the dawn wind brought them forgetfulness, so that their pleasure in the small joys of daily business would not be spoiled by remembrance of an experience that dwarfed and diminished them.[7]

Like and not like. Capable of being imaged, and incapable of being known.

On very bad days, we might try placing ourselves at the center of a particularly galling problem, or a person seemingly without hope. We rest simply at that point which I have called the mystery of resolution. We do not ask to see the how of it; we do not construct its details. We wait there, open to transformation, letting its Easter penetrate every crevice of our suspicion and despair.

There is also the prayer of freedom. We have run the fingers of our acceptance along walls, hedges, and chains. Each day's

[7]Kenneth Grahame. *The Wind in the Willows* (Scribners, N.Y., 1961).

sun has sunk into the mystery of its own limitation. But on the far side of the most inexorable limitation of all—our mortality—waits our created share in the limitless meaning of life. I will not say that there all limitations will evaporate. This wouldn't be true, for one thing, and I am too fond of a lot of them for another. We will still be creatures, however deep our participation in the limitlessness of our creator, but there our limitation will be our pleasure and our glory. And whatever in it has cramped, disappointed, denied the endless quality of our desire will be gone. Eternity has no translation of the word "No."

Perhaps it will be still an exploration, a shaded curving road with unsuspected vistas and companionable brooks around the next turn and the next. But however our freedom comes, we shall be free. I admit that here my own imagination falters. I can believe in it, hope in it, know very well that it is so, but I cannot imagine it. I can, however, sit quietly in the incapacity of my imagination, stand on its last white beach. We shall be free.

> Bred as we, among the mountains,
> Can the sailor understand
> The divine intoxication
> Of the first league out from land?